SRA Reading Mastery Plus

Teacher's Guide

Level 4

Siegfried Engelmann
Susan Hanner

SRA
A Division of The McGraw-Hill Companies

Columbus, Ohio

Acknowledgments

The authors are grateful to the following people for their input in the field-testing and preparation of Level 4.

Laurie Anders

Sandy Bayless

Christina Falkenberg

Pat Pielaet

Mary Rosenbaum

Peggy Peterson

www.sra4kids.com

SRA/McGraw-Hill

A Division of The McGraw·Hill Companies

Send all inquiries to:
SRA/McGraw-Hill
8787 Orion Place
Columbus, OH 43240-4027

Printed in the United States of America.

ISBN 0-07-569150-7

3 4 5 6 7 8 9 POH 06 05 04 03 02

Contents

Which *Reading Mastery* Program Is Right for Your Students?

Reading Mastery Plus, Level 4, is used as part of the *Reading Mastery Plus* option and as part of the *Reading Mastery Rainbow* option. The difference between the Plus option and the Rainbow option is simply the number of components that are included in the program. The Plus option is a language-arts program. The Rainbow option is a core reading program that does not have all the components that are in the Plus option. Below is a comparison of the components that are used for the Rainbow option and the Plus option. If you are using a program strictly as a reading program, you would use all the components specified in the first column. If you wish to use additional components of Plus, they are available and are indicated as being "Optional for Rainbow." So if you select the Rainbow option, your program will consist of everything in the first column. If you want to expand it, you may select from the options in the second column. If you select the *Reading Mastery Plus* option, all the components in the second column are included.

The pages that follow in this guide are based on the Plus option and assume that all the components are used. If you're using the Rainbow option, skip those parts of the guide that refer to the optional language-arts components. These are the boldfaced items shown in the second column.

Level 4

Reading Mastery Rainbow 4
Two Presentation Books
Answer Key
Teacher's Guide
Two Textbooks
Two Workbooks

Reading Mastery Plus 4
Two Presentation Books
Answer Key
Teacher's Guide
Two Textbooks
Two Workbooks

OPTIONAL FOR RAINBOW
Language Arts Guide
Activities Across the Curriculum
Literature Guide
Literature Anthology

Introduction

Reading Mastery Plus Level 4 is a one-year program containing 140 lessons that are designed to follow *Reading Mastery Plus* Level 3. All levels of *Reading Mastery Plus* are research-based sequences that have been thoroughly field-tested and revised on the basis of performance of teachers and students.

Following completion of *Reading Mastery Plus* Level 4, students may go into a variety of programs. They may continue with structured reading. One such option, which is continuous with the skills and formats of Level 4, is *Reading Mastery Plus* Level 5.

In any case, the students who complete Level 4 will have solid decoding skills, a relatively large reading vocabulary, and a good working knowledge of word meanings. The most important attribute students will have, however, is skill in **reading to learn.** They will be well-practiced in learning new concepts and gleaning new information from texts that they read, rather than from accompanying discussions. Their ability to "read to learn" enables them to engage in a variety of sophisticated projects involving research and reading on a variety of topics.

Many students who fail to become good functional readers have not received the kind of practice and perspectives necessary to develop proficiency in reading to learn. Their reading programs concentrated almost exclusively on stories, simple information passages, and literature.

In contrast, *Reading Mastery Plus* Level 4 provides a very strong focus on the skills needed for students to become proficient at letting a textbook or article "teach" them something that may involve rules and evidence.

Facts About the Program

For Whom

Reading Mastery Plus Level 4 is appropriate for students who have completed *Reading Mastery Plus* Level 3. It also may be used for any student who reads at about beginning fourth-grade level. The placement test that appears in Appendix A of this guide may be used to determine whether students meet the criteria for placement in *Reading Mastery Plus* Level 4.

Program Components

Teacher Support

The following teacher materials are included in *Reading Mastery Plus* Level 4:

- **2 presentation books** provide specific teacher instructions for presenting every activity in the program.

- **An Answer Key book** contains answer keys for worksheet and textbook responses.

- **The Teacher's Guide** provides a complete explanation of the program and how to teach it. Explanations of the program components indicate skills students learn. The guide provides suggestions for teaching critical exercises and for correcting more typical mistakes. The guide also discusses the in-program tests and specifies remedies for students who do not perform acceptably on these tests. The guide's Appendices include a list of special projects, glossaries, placement test, and reproducible

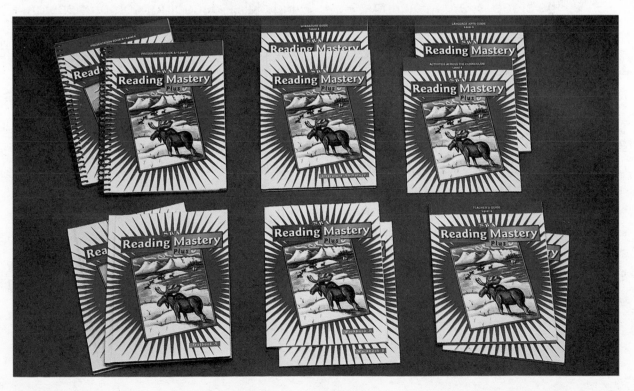

blackline masters used in teaching the program. It also contains two blackline masters of family letters to be sent home at the beginning and end of the school year.

- **The Literature Guide** provides directions and blackline masters for activities that are specified for the 17 literature selections that students read and the 3 "read-to" selections. For most literature lessons, students learn the new vocabulary that is in the selection, read the selection, answer questions, and do one or more expansion activities.

- **The Language Arts Guide** provides directions and blackline masters for the further developement of selected reading-related skills. These exercises run every day in the program.

- **Activities Across the Curriculum** provides directions and blackline masters for 33 activities that can be used throughout the program to extend and reinforce the skills the students are acquiring.

Student Materials

The following student materials are included in *Reading Mastery Plus* Level 4:

- **2 textbooks** with 4-color illustrations contain vocabulary lists, stories, and information passages that students read as part of every reading lesson, comprehension items for the stories and the information passages presented in the lessons, and tests 1–14.

- **Worksheets for daily lessons** provide additional comprehension activities, which are coordinated with the textbook stories.

- **A literature anthology** is used in the 15 literature lessons to reinforce the skills students learn in the reading program and to enrich their experiences with literature.

- **Blackline masters** appearing in this guide, in the Literature Guide, and in the Language Arts Guide are to be reproduced for fact-game activities, literature-lesson activities, and other selected reading-related skills.

Scheduling Lessons

The program includes daily reading lessons and (starting at lesson 1 and continuing through lesson 140) daily lessons for reading-related skills. The program also includes intermittent project lessons and literature lessons.

Daily reading lessons require 35 to 40 minutes each. They address core reading skills—decoding, comprehension, and skills in "reading to learn." The anticipated rate is that students complete one lesson per day.

Daily independent-work periods require 30 minutes each. Students need this in-school time to complete the independent work presented in the daily reading lessons.

Each project lesson and literature lesson requires 40 to 80 minutes; however, some projects could require even more time. These lessons should not be scheduled as part of the daily reading period, but should occur at other times.

Each lesson in the Language Arts Guide requires up to 20 minutes. The lessons provide time for students to complete independent work and for the workcheck of that work. These lessons should not be scheduled in the 40 minutes allowed for the daily reading lesson.

The time required to complete the activities in *Activities Across the Curriculum* varies from approximately 10 minutes to about an hour. These activities should be scheduled outside of the daily reading lesson.

Also, a daily workcheck period of 10 minutes is highly desirable. This time could be scheduled at a time other than the reading period or could be added to the beginning of the reading period (making the reading period 45 to 50 minutes per day).

An efficient scheduling option has a daily 35 to 40-minute period in the morning for presenting the regular reading lesson and a daily 25-minute period in the afternoon devoted to language arts and a workcheck of the students' independent work.

The chart below summarizes the time requirements for teaching *Reading Mastery Plus* Level 4 effectively:

Time needed	Lesson type	How often
40 minutes	Reading lesson	Daily
30 minutes	Independent-work	Daily
up to 20 minutes	Language arts lesson	Daily
10 minutes	Workcheck	Daily
40 to 80 minutes	Project lesson	For every major story sequence
10 to 60 minutes	Activity lesson	From time to time
40 to 80 minutes	Literature lesson	Every 10 lessons

Lesson Types

Reading Mastery Plus Level 4 has seven lesson types. Some are main lessons, and some are supplemental. The following chart summarizes the lesson types:

Only the main reading lessons are to be presented during the daily 40-minute reading periods. All other lessons—literature, language arts activity and special-project lessons—are to be presented during some other time of the school day.

Main Lessons (1–140):	
Number	Type
113	Reading lessons (lessons 1–9, 11–14, 16–19, 21–24, etc.).
13	Reading lessons plus individual reading checkouts (every 10 lessons: 15, 25, 35, etc.).
14	Test lessons (every 10 lessons: 10, 20, 30, etc. Test lessons include individual reading checkouts.).
Supplemental Lessons (1–140):	
140	Language arts lessons (part of every reading lesson)
15	Literature lessons (following every tenth lesson: 10, 20, etc, plus lesson 135.).
12	Special project lessons (following every major story sequence).
33	Activity lessons (from time to time).

Reading Lessons

The teaching structures of the 140 numbered reading lessons fall into three types.

1. The first is the **regular reading lesson,** which generally consists of word attack exercises, vocabulary exercises, and one or more selections that students read during the period.

2. The second lesson type consists of a **regular reading lesson, plus a reading checkout,** during which students individually read a 100-word passage from the preceding lesson.

3. The third type of reading lesson is the **test lesson,** which occurs every tenth lesson. The test lesson assesses the students' performance on both the content presented in the preceding nine lessons, and rate and accuracy in reading a 100-word passage. Students also play a fact game as part of the test lesson. The facts are taken from the preceding nine lessons.

Literature Lessons

Literature lessons present stories, poems, and a play.

These lessons occur every tenth lesson, starting with lesson 10, plus lesson 135. Literature lessons generally require a time period of 40 to 80 minutes, and may require more than one day to complete. The scheduled reading periods should **not** be used for presenting literature lessons.

During most literature lessons students read a selection, respond to comprehension questions about the selection, and do related activities, which may include conducting further research or engaging in a class project.

Special-Project Lessons

The 12 special-project lessons occur intermittently, usually after students complete a major story sequence in the reading program. The special projects and the necessary materials are listed in Appendix B. The projects include making a dinosaur wall chart, training an animal to do a trick, and completing a scavenger hunt. The work on each project derives from rules and information that students have already mastered in the reading lessons. Some projects may require more than 80 minutes, and may take more than one day to complete. Some projects may require using computers to answer specific questions that are difficult to research through encyclopedias. (Web sites such as Ask.com are able to handle almost any question.) Some projects may be started in class and then completed as homework assignments.

The special projects expand on the unique emphases of each major story sequence. The special projects:
(1) provide students with information that amplifies rules or perspectives presented in main stories; (2) provide experience with cooperative learning; (3) give students an opportunity to work independently at finding information; (4) engage students in activities that reinforce self-expression.

The cycle guarantees that students learn that information applies to different contexts, that information serves as a basis for drawing inferences, and that comprehension and enjoyment of stories increases when inferences are drawn.

Language Arts Lessons

Daily lessons are presented from the Language Arts Guide. These require up to 20 minutes per lesson. Most lessons involve the use of blackline masters that need to be reproduced. These lessons should be presented at a time other than that scheduled for the daily reading lesson.

Activity Lessons

The lessons provide 33 activities, most of which have blackline master student material. Each activity is keyed to a specific lesson range in *Reading Mastery Plus* Level 4. The activities cover a range of content areas, including science, social studies, and geography.

Each activity expands on the skills or information presented in the specified lessons of *Reading Mastery Plus* Level 4. Each activity specifies the content area being explored, materials required, and the objective.

To use the program:

- Select the activities that you wish to present and schedule them at a time when the students have completed the targeted lessons in *Reading Mastery Plus* Level 4.

- Schedule sufficient time for the activity, but don't allow so much time that activity work seriously impedes students' progress through *Reading Mastery Plus* Level 4.

- Provide students with copies of blackline masters required for most activities.

Lesson Events

The 5-lesson planning pages show the specific lesson events for each lesson.

The following chart summarizes the lesson events for the different types of reading lessons—regular lessons, checkout lessons, and test lessons. The events

Lesson Events	Regular Lesson	Checkout Lesson	Test Lesson
Oral vocabulary practice	(X)	(X)	
Word-attack presentation	X	X	
Comprehension passage	(X)	(X)	
Main-story reading	X	X	
Paired practice	X		
Independent work	X	X	
Workcheck	X	X	
Individual reading checkout		X	X
Fact game			X
Test of program content			X
Fact review	(X)	(X)	

are listed in the order of their occurrence during the lesson. Xs indicate which events occur in lessons. Xs in parentheses indicate that the lesson event does not occur in every lesson. For example, the parentheses around the Xs for **comprehension passage** indicate that the comprehension passages do not appear in every lesson; however, when they do appear, they are presented immediately before the main-story reading.

Here is a summary of the events for **regular lessons:**

• **Oral vocabulary practice**—teacher directed. Students learn and review words and expressions that will be used in later reading selections.

• **Word-attack presentation**—teacher directed. The students read lists of words aloud and do word-meaning activities with some of the words.

• **Comprehension passage**—teacher directed. The students orally read a short passage that presents information to be used in later reading activities. The students orally respond to specified tasks about key details of the comprehension passage.

• **Main-story reading**—teacher directed. Main stories are the primary teacher-directed activity in every regular lesson. The students orally read a long selection (between 250 and 950 words) and orally respond to specific comprehension tasks the teacher presents. Beginning with lesson 13, students silently read between 50 and 400 words for each lesson. All main stories have more than one part. Parts are presented

on consecutive regular lessons. Some main stories (such as Al and Angela) span more than 10 lessons. The story comprehension items refer to earlier parts as well as the part presented in the current lesson.

• **Paired practice.** This activity is part of each regular lesson. It occurs immediately after the reading of the main story. Students work in pairs and read half of that story to their partner. For paired practice, students are permanently assigned as either the A member or the B member of the pair. On alternate days, the A member reads the first part of the specified passage, and the B member reads the second part.

• **Independent work.** Students write answers to written items relating to (a) the comprehension passage, (b) the main story, (c) previously taught content, and (d) skills that students have learned (vocabulary words, sequencing, etc.). For typical lessons, some independent work appears on the student worksheet and some in the student textbook.

• **Workcheck**—teacher directed. The teacher (a) checks the students' independent work and (b) makes sure the students understand and correct the items they missed.

Checkout lessons occur every tenth lesson, starting with lesson 10. Students individually read a passage from the main story that was presented in the preceding lesson. Checkout lessons are designed to give the students practice in meeting rate and accuracy criteria for oral reading.

Test lessons occur every tenth lesson, starting with lesson 10. Test lessons consist of items that test students' comprehension of the new vocabulary, information, rules, and other skills that were presented in the preceding nine lessons. The lessons also present a rate-and-accuracy checkout on a one-hundred-word passage from the preceding lesson.

Students also play a **fact game** in test lessons. These games provide students with practice on important facts presented in the preceding nine lessons.

Grouping the Students

If the ability level of students in the classroom is fairly homogeneous, *Reading Mastery Plus* Level 4 may be presented to the entire class. One problem with large entire-class instruction is that the individual students do not receive as many opportunities to read aloud. For this reason, you may decide to place the most able students in one group and the lower performers in another group. All students now receive more practice with supervised reading.

The placement test that appears in Appendix A of this guide may be used to evaluate each student's entry level. Directions for administering the test and criteria for placing students in the program accompany the test.

Overview of Decoding and Comprehension Emphases

Each lesson in *Reading Mastery Plus* Level 4 has two distinct objectives: one is decoding, the other is comprehension. The word-attack presentation deals not only with teaching decoding skills, but also with developing understanding of key words. Similarly, the comprehension passage and the main story are not simply vehicles for comprehension; important decoding objectives are also met through these activities.

The following outline summarizes the activities involved in the development of decoding rate and accuracy and the development of various comprehension skills. The outline specifies the part of the lesson or the material that develops each subskill.

I. DECODING EMPHASIS

A. *Word-Attack Exercises* (presented during the first part of each lesson)

1. *New hard words* are modeled by the teacher and then decoded by the students.

2. *Words with similar features* (for example, all end in **S,** all have an ending, or all are compound words) are grouped together in columns and are read by the students.

3. *Unrelated decodable words* (those that have been presented earlier or those that should be decodable by virtue of the students' skills) are grouped in columns.

B. *Main-Story Reading Procedures* (presented with the main selection for each lesson)

1. Students orally read two or three sentences for each turn.

2. Corrections for decoding errors are provided immediately. The teacher identifies the missed word, and the student rereads the sentence in which the word appears.

3. Students read the last part of the selection silently (starting in lesson 13).

Note: Procedures 1 and 2 also apply to the comprehension passage.

C. *Paired Practice*

Permanently assigned pairs of students orally reread the main story to each other. Partners are to correct each other's decoding errors.

D. *Fifth-Lesson Individual Reading Checkouts*

Students individually read a one-hundred-word passage selected from the main story of the preceding lesson and meet a specified rate-accuracy criterion.

II. COMPREHENSION EMPHASIS

A. *Vocabulary Model Sentences*
Selected vocabulary words appear in sentences like "He <u>responded</u> to her <u>clever</u> <u>solution</u>."

1. Students learn what each sentence means and practice saying the sentence.

2. Students respond to tasks about the meaning of specific words.

B. *Word-Attack*

Critical vocabulary items (idioms, phrases, and individual words that will appear in stories or comprehension passages) are pretaught. The teacher tells the meaning of each vocabulary word or models how to use it.

C. *Comprehension-Passage Reading*
(These passages preteach information that will appear in main stories.)

1. As the students read each passage aloud, the teacher presents specified comprehension tasks.

2. The students respond orally.

D. *Main-Story Reading Activities*

1. As the students read the story, the teacher presents specified comprehension tasks. The students respond orally.

2. The teacher presents a variety of tasks requiring recall of information, application of rules, inferences based on specific facts, and inferences based on information about different characters.

E. *Independent-Work Applications*

The students independently write answers to items that appear on the worksheets and in the textbook.

1. Some items relate to the main story that the group read.

2. If the lesson contains a comprehension passage, some items relate to the information presented in that passage.

3. Some items relate to skills (such as sequencing story events and vocabulary meanings).

4. Review items present information from earlier main stories or comprehension passages.

F. *Daily Workcheck*

1. Independent work is checked.

2. Students receive same-day feedback on their independent-work performance. (They receive information on the correct answers to all items.)

G. *Tenth-Lesson Fact Games*

1. The students play a game in which they orally respond to comprehension items.

2. These comprehension items cover key concepts and facts from earlier lessons. The items are particularly important because they will recur in later lessons.

H. *Tenth-Lesson Tests*

Students write answers to items that deal with rules, vocabulary meanings, and information presented in the preceding nine lessons.

The Decoding Emphasis

The decoding emphasis involves a cycle that introduces new decoding words and word families, presents these words in different story contexts, and provides practice in meeting oral reading rate-accuracy criteria. Both the decoding vocabulary and the various decoding-practice activities are coordinated in word-attack presentations, in group story readings, and, finally, in individual reading checkouts.

Students read selections that are composed entirely of words or decodable elements taught earlier in *Reading Mastery Plus* Level 4.

The Cycle for Developing Decoding Skills

The cycle for introducing a decoding word in *Reading Mastery Plus* Level 4 begins with the word appearing in the word-attack lists on one or more lessons. Then the word appears in reading selections. This development of decoding words ensures that students receive practice in reading words in sentence contexts after these words have been presented in lists.

Word-Attack Presentation

The first decoding activity in every lesson is the word-attack presentation, during which the students read about 5 to 25 words aloud.

• For words that appeared earlier or that are decodable the teacher asks, What word?

• Words that would probably be difficult to read are first modeled by the teacher, then read by the students. Some words are also spelled. For example: Word 1 is **actually**. What word? *Actually.* Spell **actually**. *A-C-T-U-A-L-L-Y.*

• To show students structural or phonemic similarities of different word families, the teacher presents groups of words that have common features. On page 17 are the word-attack words from lesson 41. Note that the words in columns 3 and 4 have endings, and the words in column 2 are compound words.

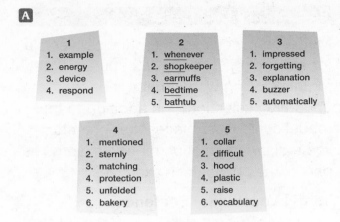

A

1	2	3
1. example	1. whenever	1. impressed
2. energy	2. shopkeeper	2. forgetting
3. device	3. earmuffs	3. explanation
4. respond	4. bedtime	4. buzzer
	5. bathtub	5. automatically

4	5
1. mentioned	1. collar
2. sternly	2. difficult
3. matching	3. hood
4. protection	4. plastic
5. unfolded	5. raise
6. bakery	6. vocabulary

- For each word whose meaning may not be familiar to the students, the teacher gives an explanation of the meaning. Below is the teacher presentation script for column 4 of the word-attack exercise.

Column 4

t. Find column 4. ✓
- (Teacher reference:)

> 1. **mentioned**   4. **protection**
> 2. **sternly**   5. **unfolded**
> 3. **matching**   6. **bakery**

- All these words have an ending.
u. Word 1. What word? (Signal.) *Mentioned.*
- When you mention something, you quickly tell about it. Everybody, what's another way of saying **quickly tell?** (Signal.) *Mention.*
v. Word 2. What word? (Signal.) *Sternly.*
- A stern expression is a frowning expression. Here's a stern expression. (Frown.)
w. Word 3. What word? (Signal.) *Matching.*
- (Repeat for words 4–6.)
x. Let's read those words again.
- Word 1. What word? (Signal.) *Mentioned.*
- (Repeat for words 2–6.)
y. (Repeat step x until firm.)

Main-Story Decoding

Following the word-attack part of the lesson, the group reads the comprehension passage and all or part of the main story aloud. As students progress through the program, less of the main story is read aloud. At first, they read only about 50 words silently. Later, they read 400 words or more.

The teacher calls on individual students to take turns, each reading two or three sentences. Every main story has an **error limit** based on two errors per hundred words in the story. If the group exceeds the error limit, the students are to reread the main story until they read within the specified error limit.

The main stories contain recently introduced words. The stories, therefore, provide word-recognition practice with these words. The error limit for the story helps the students develop effective strategies for learning new words: (1) The students quickly learn that words appearing in the word-attack lists will appear in main stories, (2) They learn that if they are to read the stories within the error limits, they should pay attention to these words when they appear in the lists.

Paired-Reading Practice

The purpose of paired reading is to provide students with an opportunity to read a relatively long passage without interruption. Although students receive oral-reading practice during the main-story reading, they usually read only two or three sentences at a time, and their reading may be interrupted with comprehension items. The paired-reading practice takes 10 to 12 minutes for each lesson and makes a marked difference in the fluency performance of students.

Individual Reading Checkouts

Every fifth lesson includes a reading checkout, beginning with lesson 10. Students individually read a one-hundred-word passage to a checker. The purpose of the checkout is to ensure that students are progressing acceptably in oral decoding rate and accuracy. The passage that they read for the checkout is taken from the preceding lesson. To pass the checkout, the student reads the passage in less than a minute and makes no more than two errors.

The Comprehension Emphasis

Reading Mastery Plus Level 4 has a comprehension emphasis on the facts and rules that are presented in what the students read. The program also has a vocabulary-building emphasis.

Vocabulary Emphasis

Model sentences are the principal vehicle for expanding students' vocabulary and for introducing words that will be in upcoming selections. In addition to the model sentences, the teacher presents vocabulary information for some words as part of the word-attack exercises.

Model Vocabulary Sentences

The first model sentence is introduced in lesson 3. Others follow about every four lessons. A list of sentences appears in the back of the student textbooks (and Appendix C of this guide). Students refer to this list when learning new sentences.

Each model sentence goes through a seven-step cycle.

1. The sentence is introduced. Students read the sentence. The teacher explains the key words (two to four new words that are in the sentence). Then students answer questions about the key words. For example, for the sentence **Scientists do not ignore ordinary things** the teacher asks these questions:

   What word means that you don't pay attention to something?

   What word tells about things that you see all the time?

   What do we call highly trained people who study different things about the world?

2. In the following lesson, students review the model sentence.

3. In the third lesson of the cycle, students review the last three model sentences that had been introduced.

4. Later in that lesson, students do written tasks in which they write answers to questions about the key words.

5. In the next lesson, the teacher says part of the sentence but stops just before a key word. Students say the next word.

6. Later in that lesson, students work with the two most recent sentences, which are presented with key words missing. Students write the complete sentences. (For example, the model sentence would appear as: ■■ do not ■■ ■■ things.)

7. The test in every tenth lesson contains skill items that assess the students' knowledge of vocabulary words presented in the model sentences that were introduced and sufficiently reviewed during the preceding nine lessons.

Vocabulary During Word Attack

The teacher script provides "definitions" for those words that students may not know. These descriptions often show the students how to use the word. There is no attempt to provide students with **a variety of meanings of the word,** but merely to illustrate the meaning that will be used in the upcoming selection.

Here are some examples:

> **Shallow. Shallow** is the opposite of **deep.** What's the opposite of **a deep bowl?** (Signal.) *A shallow bowl.*

> **Practice.** When you **practice** something, you work at it. What's another way of saying **He worked on throwing a ball?** (Signal.) *He practiced throwing a ball.*

Definitions for all vocabulary words appear in Appendix D of this guide and in a glossary at the end of each textbook.

Developing Comprehension of Facts, Rules, and Perspectives

As decoding skills are being developed through the various lesson activities, comprehension skills are also being developed for interpreting and using facts, rules, and information about unique story-character perspectives. The general skills students learn include cause and effect, literal meaning, inferential meaning, main idea, and sequencing of events. The program presents content and practice for these skills.

Here is a summary of the sequence for developing these skills:

1. Information is introduced in a comprehension passage.

2. Within two lessons of the introduction, the information is used in the main story.

3. A variation of the information also appears in the independent-work items.

4. Some of the items are reviewed in subsequent lessons.

5. Information that is particularly important or difficult appears in the fact games or in fact reviews. The game format provides the students with massed practice on a lot of information.

6. The tenth-lesson tests assess students' understanding of the information.

7. The final step is the integration of recent information with information taught earlier. This integration provides for increasingly complex applications and review. For major story sequences, the integration culminates with a special project, in which students research additional facets of the story theme.

General Comprehension Skills

The comprehension skills that are traditionally presented in developmental reading series stress general skills such as literal comprehension, main idea, fact versus opinion, context clues, and sequencing of events. *Reading Mastery Plus* Level 4 is organized so that these skills are taught in a cumulative manner, which means that a particular skill is practiced not merely as a part of a few lessons, but is practiced repeatedly as part of many lessons. This cumulative practice ensures that the students work with the various skills in a variety of story and information contexts.

The table on page 21 summarizes the comprehension skills emphasized in each of the larger story series in *Reading Mastery Plus* Level 4. (Each story series listed spans at least three lessons.) The lesson numbers for each series are indicated in the table. If the series strongly emphasizes a particular skill, the skill is marked with a star (☆). If the emphasis is not as strong, it is marked with a checkmark (✓).

As the table shows, literal comprehension, cause and effect, supporting evidence, sequencing, context clues, viewpoint, character development, reference–book skills, and information recall activities are part of each story series. In addition to

providing practice in these categories of comprehension skills, each story series has at least one strong focus. For example, the series about Leonard (a boy who invents something) presents strong comprehension emphasis on sequencing, context clues, viewpoint, supporting evidence, cause and effect, character development, reference-book skills, and information recall.

Facts and Rules

The information presented in *Reading Mastery Plus* Level 4 covers a very broad range of topics. However, the goal of the program is to develop information so that individual facts are related to other facts in a way that provides students with a fact perspective.

Three major fact perspectives are developed in *Reading Mastery Plus* Level 4. These deal with **places,** with **common material in the environment,** and with **people.**

Places

The scheme for developing a perspective for places involves introducing geographic information about different places, teaching about land forms associated with those places, teaching about the animals that live in the places, and providing information on unique details of the place or the things that are observed in the place.

The diagram below shows the organization of material for the place perspective.

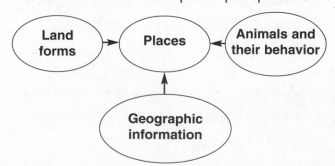

Table of Cumulative Comprehension Emphasis

☆ = Strong
✔ = Not as strong

	1–12 (Old Henry)	13–22 (Oomoo & Oolak)	24–35 (Edna & Carla)	36–51 (Leonard)	53–66 (Wendy)	67–84 (Waldo)	85–90 (Darla)	91–100 (Iditarod)	101–140 (Al & Angela)
Literal Comprehension	✔	✔	✔	✔	✔	✔	✔	✔	✔
Supporting evidence (relevant details)	✔	☆	☆	☆	✔	☆	☆	☆	✔
Main idea				✔		✔	☆	☆	☆
Information recall	☆	☆	☆	☆	☆	☆	☆	☆	☆
Sequencing	☆	☆	☆	☆	☆	☆	☆	✔	☆
Cause and effect	☆	☆	☆	☆	☆	☆	☆	☆	☆
Facts vs. opinion		✔	☆	✔		✔	✔	☆	
Context clues	✔	☆	☆	☆	✔	✔	☆	☆	✔
Viewpoint	☆	☆	☆	☆	☆	☆	☆	☆	☆
Character development (inferring motives and predicting behavior)	☆	✔	✔	☆	☆	☆	☆	☆	☆
Map skills	☆	☆	✔		✔	✔	✔	✔	☆
Reference-book skills	☆	✔	✔	☆	☆	☆	✔	☆	☆

Below is a list of the major places and related information presented in *Reading Mastery Plus* Level 4.

Places	Land forms	Animals and their behavior
Japan	Rocky Mountains	Polar bears
Tokyo	Ice floes	Killer whales
Canada	Polar caps	Walruses
Alaska	Volcanos	Seals
The poles	Earthquakes	Dinosaurs
Equator		Baboons
Solar system		Squid
Galaxies	**Geographic information**	Blue whales
Pacific Ocean	Facts about:	Pigeons
Atlantic Ocean	mountains	Rabbits
Bermuda Islands	ice floes	Dogs
Andros Island	the polar caps	Geese
Bermuda Triangle	volcanos	Sled dogs
Florida	earthquakes	
Colorado		
Utah		
Africa		
Michigan		
Kentucky		

Common Materials

The perspective for common materials is developed by introducing common material and then presenting facts and rules that explain the way the material behaves. For example, air and water are common materials. The students are introduced to facts and rules that explain how these materials behave in different settings (how air turns into a solid if it is cooled enough; how water exerts great pressure if you are far underwater).

Below is a diagram for the development of the common materials perspective.

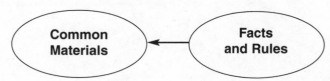

The major common-material topics developed in *Reading Mastery Plus* Level 4 are:

Water　　　　**Clouds**

Air　　　　　**Sun**

Snowflakes

People

The perspective developed for people proceeds in two different directions. One direction involves character development. For example, information presented about a character is used to predict how that character will behave in a new situation. The other direction involves facts about the body systems of humans and how they work—muscles, bones, heart, and so on.

The diagram below shows how the people perspective is developed.

Below is a list of the major people-perspective topics developed in *Reading Mastery Plus* Level 4.

Character	Body systems
Motives	Muscles
Predictable behaviors	Eyes
Comparison of verbal	Bones
behavior with actual	Nerves
behavior	Heart
	Brain
	Spinal cord
	Lungs
	Blood vessels
	Ears

Preparing to Teach

This section of the guide provides you with specific, technical information about what you will be teaching and some of the problems students may have with the presentations. The purpose is to provide you with the information and the general cautions you need to **guarantee** that the students move through the program smoothly.

The guide is a tool that you should refer to throughout the year as part of your preparation for teaching the program.

1. Don't begin the program until you have studied this section of the guide.

2. Practice presenting the various exercises before you present the first lessons to the students. Don't simply read them over and assume that you will be able to present them well. Read the script aloud. Present the signals the students are to respond to. Practice saying the corrections. Make sure you can smoothly present any new exercise type that is scheduled for upcoming lessons. During the first part of the program, a fair amount of practice may be required. For later lessons, less preparation is needed.

General Teaching Strategies

When teaching *Reading Mastery Plus* Level 4 you will be engaged in various types of activities.

- You will present model sentences and word-attack exercises.

- You will direct the students in the group reading of comprehension passages and main stories. (As they read, you will present specified oral comprehension tasks.)

- You will monitor students as they do their independent work.

- You will provide a daily workcheck and record the number of errors students make on their independent work.

- For lessons that involve individual checkouts and fact games, you will monitor the checkouts and games.

- You will provide remedies for students who do not pass tenth-lesson tests.

Here is a summary of the general techniques that you will use.

Get into the lesson quickly. No discussions are necessary.

Teach to mastery. Use the following guidelines:

- Repeat tasks if students are not firm.

- Use clear signals. All signals have the same purpose: They trigger a simultaneous response from the group. All signals have the same rationale: If you get the group to respond simultaneously (with no student leading the others) you will receive good information about the performance of the students. At the same time, students will receive more frequent practice than they would using individual responses.

- Reinforce good performance. Make your praise specific. If the students have just completed a difficult word list with no errors tell them what they did: You read without any mistakes. Good for you. Praise students for following the rules you present.

Pace the exercises. Since a great deal of information must be taught during the daily presentation, it is important for you to move quickly, but not to rush the students so much that they make mistakes. To ensure a smoothly paced lesson, you should become familiar with the exercises before presenting them. You must be able to present them without having to refer to the page for every word. Fast pacing is important for the following reasons:

- It reduces the problems of managing students and maintaining on-task behavior. Studies have shown that faster pacing secures more student interest and reduces management problems.

- Fast pacing results in greater student achievement. With faster pacing, a teacher can cover more material in a fixed amount of time and provide more student practice in that time.

- Many tasks become more difficult when they are presented slowly. Slower pacing places greater memory demands on students. Faster pacing, on the other hand, reduces memory load.

Monitor independent work. Intermittently monitor students as they do their independent work. Make sure that students are working at a reasonable rate, but are not looking up answers to items and are not copying.

Using the Teacher-Presentation Scripts

The script for each lesson indicates how to present the structured activities. The lesson is a script that shows what you say, what you do, and what the students' responses are to be.

What you say appears in blue type:

You say this.

What you do appears in parentheses:

(You do this.)

The responses of the students are in italics:

Students say this.

[Individual student says this.]

Follow the specified wording in the script. While wording variations from the script are not always dangerous, you will be assured of communicating clearly with the students if you follow the script exactly. The wording in the teacher presentation books is succinctly controlled. The tasks are arranged so they focus on important aspects of what the students are to do. Although you may initially feel uncomfortable "reading" from a script, follow the scripts very closely; try to present them as if you're saying something important to the students. If you do, you'll soon find that working from a script is not difficult and that students indeed respond well to what you say.

Conventions

Samples of the teacher presentation script appear on page 26.

The arrows show the six different things you'll do that are not spelled out in the script. You'll signal to make sure that group responses involve all the students. You'll "firm" critical parts of the exercises. For some exercises, you'll write things on the board.

Arrow ❶: Signals for Group Responses
(Signal.) and (Tap.)

Some tasks call for group responses. If students respond together with brisk, unison responses, you receive good information about whether the students are performing correctly. The simplest way to direct students to respond together is to signal or tap in a predictable cadence— just like the cadence in a musical piece. By listening carefully to the responses, you can tell both which students make mistakes and which ones respond late, copying those who responded first. As a result, you are able to correct specific mistakes, maximize the amount of practice, and evaluate the performance of each student.

Arrows labeled 1 on page 26 specify (Signal.) for the student responses **thun, thunder,** and taps for the student spelling of **thunder** (a series of responses).

Using Signals

To signal the group to respond:

1. Say the task specified in the presentation script.

2. Pause.

3. Clap, or make another auditory signal such as a tap or a finger snap. (An auditory signal is necessary because the students are not looking at you but at the material they are reading.)

Here are procedures for effective signaling:

- Don't signal while talking. Talk first, then signal.

- Always maintain a time interval of about one second between the last word of the instructions or question and the signal. Signal timing should be consistent so students can respond together.

- Require students to respond together, on signal.

Column 1

a. **Find lesson 27 in your textbook.** ✓ ← ❸
- Touch column 1. ✓
- (Teacher reference:) ← ❺

1. <u>thun</u>der	4. <u>some</u>how
2. <u>shal</u>low	5. <u>light</u>ning
3. <u>blind</u>ing	

- All these words have more than one syllable. The first syllable of each word is underlined.

b. Word 1. What's the first syllable? (Signal.) *thun.*
- What's the whole word? (Signal.) ← ❶ *Thunder.*
- Spell **thunder.** Get ready. (Tap for each letter.) *T-H-U-N-D-E-R.*

c. Word 2. What's the first syllable? (Signal.) *Shall.*
- What's the whole word? (Signal.) *Shallow.*
- Spell **shallow.** Get ready. (Tap for each letter.) *S-H-A-L-L-O-W.*

d. Word 3. What's the first syllable? (Signal.) *blind.*
- What's the whole word? (Signal.) *Blinding.*
- Spell **blinding.** Get ready. (Tap for each letter.) *B-L-I-N-D-I-N-G.*

e. Word 4. What's the first syllable? (Signal.) *some.*
- What's the whole word? (Signal.) *Somehow.*
- Spell **somehow.** Get ready. (Tap for each letter.) *S-O-M-E-H-O-W.*

f. Word 5. What's the first syllable? (Signal.) *light.*
- What's the whole word? (Signal.) *Lightning.*

g. Let's read those words again.
- Word 1. What word? (Signal.) *Thunder.*
- (Repeat for words 2–5.) ← ❺

h. (Repeat step g until firm.) ← ❷

Individual Turns ← ❻

(For columns 1–4: Call on individual students, each to read one to three words per turn.)

VOCABULARY REVIEW

a. You learned a sentence that tells about the new exhibit.
- Everybody, say that sentence. Get ready. (Signal.) *The new exhibit displayed mysterious fish.*
- (Repeat until firm.) ← ❷

FACT REVIEW

a. Let's review some facts you have learned. First we'll go over the facts together. Then I'll call on individual students to do some facts.

b. Everybody, tell me how much oxygen is on Io. (Pause.) Get ready. (Signal.) *None.*
- Tell me how long it takes Io to go all the way around Jupiter. **Less than...** (Pause.) Get ready. (Signal.) *2 days.*
- Tell me which has **more** gravity—**Jupiter** or **Io.** (Pause.) Get ready. (Signal.) *Jupiter.*
- Tell me where you can jump three meters high—on Jupiter or on Io. (Pause.) Get ready. (Signal.) *On Io.*
- (Repeat step b until firm.) ← ❷

a. Find a lesson 10 on your worksheet. ✓ ← ❸
b. I'm going to say some dates. You'll write them with commas.
- Item 1: Write the date for the fifth day of August in the year 1968. When you write the date, you start with the month August, then write the number of the day, then a comma, then the number of the year Write the date August fifth, 1968 (Observe Students and give feedback.) ← ❸
- (Write on the board.)

- Check your work. Here's what you should have.

- To correct mistakes of not following the signal, show students exactly what you want them to do:

I'm good at answering the right way.

My turn: Spell **thunder.** Get ready.

(Tap) **T.** . . (tap) **H.** . . (tap) **U.** . . (tap) **N.** . . (tap) **D.** . . (tap) **E.** . . (tap) **R.**

Let's see who can do it just that way:

Your turn. Spell **thunder.** Get ready. (Tap for each letter.) *T-H-U-N-D-E-R.*

- **Do not respond with the students** unless you are trying to work with them on a difficult response. You present only what is in blue. You do not say the answers with the students, and you should not move your lips or give other nonverbal clues about what the answer is.

Signals are very important early in the program. After students have learned the routine, the signals are not as critical because the students will be able to respond on cue with no signal. That will happen, however, only if you consistently present signals with the same predictable timing.

Arrow ❷ : Firming

(Repeat until firm.)

Wherever there's a signal, there's a place where students may make mistakes. You correct mistakes as soon as you hear them. A correction may occur during any part of the teacher presentation that calls for students to respond. It may also occur in connection with what students are writing.

- Mistakes on oral responses include saying the wrong thing or not responding. To correct: **You say the correct answer; then repeat the task the students missed.** For example:

You learned a sentence about the new exhibit. Everybody, say that sentence. Get ready. (Signal.)

If some students do not respond, respond slowly, or say an incorrect sentence, a mistake has occurred. As soon as you hear a mistake, you **say the correct answer:**

Here's the sentence about the new exhibit: The new exhibit displayed mysterious fish.

Repeat the task:

Everybody, say that sentence. Get ready. (Signal.)

A special correction is needed when correcting mistakes on tasks that teach a series of things. This type of correction is marked with the notation:

(Repeat step _ until firm.)

An example of this kind of task appears on the next page. The bracket shows a section of the presentation that is to be repeated following a mistake.

EXERCISE 3

FACT REVIEW

a. Let's review some facts you have learned. First we'll go over the facts together. Then I'll call on individual students to do some facts.

b. Everybody, tell me how much oxygen is on Io. (Pause.) Get ready. (Signal.) *None.*

• Tell me how long it takes Io to go all the way around Jupiter. **Less than...** (Pause.) Get ready. (Signal.) *2 days.*

• Tell me which has **more** gravity—**Jupiter** or **Io.** (Pause.) Get ready. (Signal.) *Jupiter.*

• Tell me where you can jump three meters high—on Jupiter or on Io. (Pause.) Get ready. (Signal.) *On Io.*

• (Repeat step b until firm.) ← ❷

When you "repeat until firm," you follow these steps:

1. **Correct the mistake.** (Tell the answer and repeat the task that was missed.)

2. **Return to the beginning of the bracketed part and present the entire part.** For example, students miss the third task (Tell me which has **more** gravity—Jupiter or Io.)

   You tell the answer: Jupiter.

   You repeat the task: Tell me which has **more** gravity—Jupiter or Io.

   You return to the first task in the bracketed part and repeat the entire part: Let's go back. Tell me how much oxygen is on Io. . . etc.

Arrow ❸ : Monitoring Students
(Observe students and give feedback.) and ✔

EXERCISE 4

a. Find a lesson 10 on your worksheet. ✓ ← ❸
b. I'm going to say some dates. You'll write them with commas.
• Item 1: Write the date for the fifth day of August in the year 1968. When you write the date, you start with the month August, then write the number of the day, then a comma, then the number of the year. Write the date August fifth, 1968 (Observe Students and give feedback.) ← ❸
• (Write on the board.)

AUGUST 5, 1968 ← ❹

• Check your work. Here's what you should have.

The arrows labeled 3 show a checkmark (✔) or the direction **(Observe students and give feedback.).** These script conventions indicate how you are to monitor student performance.

The ✔ is a note to see whether the students have found or touched what you refer to. If you tell them to **turn their paper over,** or **touch column 2,** you check to see that they are doing that. Your check requires only a second or two. Monitor the responses of several "average performing" students. If their responses are acceptable, proceed with the presentation.

The **(Observe students and give feedback.)** direction implies a more elaborate response on your part. You sample more students and you give feedback, not only to individual students, but also to the group. Here are the basic rules for what to do and what not to do when you observe and give feedback:

• Circulate to make sure that you can see all of the students' papers.

- **As soon as students start to work, start observing.** As you observe, make comments to the whole class. Focus these comments on students who are following directions, working quickly, and working accurately. Wow, a couple of students are almost finished. I haven't seen one mistake so far.

- When students raise their hands to indicate that they are finished, acknowledge them.

- **If you observe mistakes, do not provide a great deal of individual help.** For example, if the directions tell students to circle the answer and some students underline it, tell them, You didn't follow the directions for number 4. Read the directions and do what they say.

If there are serious problems with part of the independent work, repeat it during the next reading period. Do not proceed in the program if the students are making a high rate of errors.

Arrow 4 : Board Work

What you write on the board is indicated in blue display boxes (see page 28). In the sample exercise, you write the date **August 5, 1968.**

Arrow 5 : Script Conventions

(Repeat for words 2–5.) and (Teacher reference:)

Sometimes teachers lose their place in the teacher presentation script. Teachers also have difficulty keeping track of where the students are supposed to be touching in their textbooks or workbooks. Arrow 5 on page 26 shows one of two script conventions that enable you to more easily track what you and the students are supposed to be doing.

In step g teachers are instructed to "Repeat for words 2–5." Teachers are to repeat: Word ___. What word? (Signal.) Repeat for the remaining words **shallow, blinding, somehow, lightning.** You don't have to read the script for those words. So you are able to attend more to what the students are doing. Here is what you would say:

g. Let's read those words again.
- Word 1. What word? (Signal.) *Thunder.*
- Word 2. What word? (Signal.) *Shallow.*
- Word 3. What word? (Signal.) *Blinding.*
- Word 4. What word? (Signal.) *Somehow.*
- Word 5. What word? (Signal.) *Lightning.*

The presentation script provides a teacher reference that shows the students' material.

5 ➞ • (Teacher reference:)

1. <u>thund</u>er	4. <u>some</u>how
2. <u>shall</u>ow	5. <u>light</u>ning
3. <u>blind</u>ing	

Refer to the teacher references as you monitor students' responses to this activity.

By looking at the teacher reference you don't have to peek at a student's textbook to see what the next word is. Using teacher references can help free you from the script without straying from the wording the script specifies. For most word lists, you'll use the same wording for all words. Once you know the wording (specified for the first word in the list) you can use the teacher reference to follow the same format shown for the first word to direct the other words.

Arrow ❻ : Individual Turns

Individual turns occur routinely as part of a word-attack presentation that has more than one column of words. Several other structured exercise types, such as fact reviews, also call for individual turns.

Think of individual turns as a diagnostic tool that lets you know if the students are firm on the material you just presented to the group. The general procedure for presenting individual turns is to present them only when you think the students are firm on the group tasks.

Call on a sufficient number of individual students to let you know whether they have mastered the content. You should not try to give every student a turn on every task, but rather you should sample the group in a way that does not consume a lot of time. If there are 25 students in the group, you might present tasks to 7 students. Of these 7, sample 4 students who may be weak on the material and 3 others. If students in this sample are firm, the others in the group are probably also firm.

Teaching to the Group

If the group has problems, you'll correct their mistakes or firm students on the content that has not been mastered. If the group is firm, you'll speed up the presentation and move on.

To adjust the presentation to the performance of the group, you have to attend to individuals within the group. Although all the students are supposed to have the skills needed to perform well in *Reading Mastery Plus* Level 4, there will be a range of individual variation.

This range in ability raises a question about whether you should adjust your presentation to the higher performers in the group, those in the middle, or the lower performers. Here are the guidelines:

- **If some students should not really be in the group** (according to their placement-test performance or performance on the lessons), **do not teach to them.** Either place them in a group that is appropriate for their performance level, or try to find a way to give them additional practice outside of the scheduled reading period. (One plan that may work is to have them read to a higher-performing student on a daily basis.)

- **If all students are appropriately placed, teach to the students who tend to be lower but who tend not to be the slowest in the group.** If you teach to the slowest, you may make the presentation tedious for most of the other students, and you will not move through the lessons as quickly as you should. If you teach to the higher performers, you will make it difficult for possibly half of the students. However, if you gauge your presentation to the performance of the lower students, you will provide a little more practice than the higher students require, but the presentation will not be significantly slowed for them. The presentation will also be careful enough that the lowest students in the group will benefit from it about 80 percent of the time. At that level, they will master the material (even if they need some additional practice).

- **Provide students with very unambiguous models of what you expect them to do.** Do not praise them for sloppy approximations, but also do not lose patience with them. Repeat material until they can perform perfectly. Unless you provide such a model, you're asking students to improve when they are not exactly sure what constitutes improvement.

- **Expect students to accelerate.** If you place students appropriately, initially teach them to a very hard criterion of performance, and show them what you expect them to do, they will learn faster and faster. Furthermore, they will enjoy learning much more.

Teaching the Lessons

This section gives information about teaching each part of the lesson.

Vocabulary Exercises

General Information

These exercises are the first in the lesson. They focus on model sentences and the meaning of several key words. The activities are oral. The expectation is that the students will perform very well on the exercises. Students should not require much time to respond, and their responses should be correct.

The exercise below is from lesson 39. The exercise introduces the vocabulary sentence: **He responded to her clever solution.** The key words are **respond, clever,** and **solution.** The focus is on the specific meaning used in the vocabulary sentence.

EXERCISE 1

VOCABULARY

a. **Find page 352 in your textbook.** ✓
- Touch sentence 9. ✓
- This is a new vocabulary sentence. It says: He responded to her clever solution. Everybody, say that sentence. Get ready. (Signal.) *He responded to her clever solution.*
- Close your eyes and say the sentence. Get ready. (Signal.) *He responded to her clever solution.*
- (Repeat until firm.)

b. The **solution** is what she did to solve a problem. What word refers to solving a problem? (Signal.) *Solution.*
c. **Responded** is another word for **reacted.** If you respond to something, you react to it.
d. Her solution was **clever.** That means it was very smart.
e. Listen to the sentence again: He responded to her clever solution. Everybody, say that sentence. Get ready. (Signal.) *He responded to her clever solution.*
f. What word means **reacted?** (Signal.) *Responded.*
- What word refers to solving a problem? (Signal.) *Solution.*
- What word means **very smart?** (Signal.) *Clever.*
- (Repeat step f until firm.)

Presenting Vocabulary Exercises

Follow these guidelines when presenting the exercises.

1. Make sure that the students produce good unison responses. Don't permit droning responses when students say the sentence.

2. Make sure that students are firm in saying the sentence. In step a, you repeat the sentence until firm. For some sentences, students may have to say it three or more times. If students are not firm in saying the sentence, however, they will have problems when the sentence is used in this lesson and reviewed in later lessons.

3. Don't make repeating the sentence seem like punishment. If you respond to these exercises as fun or challenges that you look forward to, the students will respond the same way. Keep it upbeat and fast moving: Once more. Get ready . . .

4. Make sure students are firm on what the key words mean. In step f, you present questions about the key words. If students are not perfectly firm on all the answers, they'll have problems later. So don't be afraid to repeat items that have weak responses. And don't be afraid to use individual turns for students that produce weak or questionable responses.

5. Use the vocabulary review tasks as an indicator of how well students learn the new material. The review task below is presented in the next lesson. If students do not do well on these reviews, you may need to provide more practice on the exercises that introduce the sentences.

EXERCISE 1
VOCABULARY REVIEW

a. Here's the new vocabulary sentence: He responded to her clever solution.
 • Everybody, say that sentence. Get ready. (Signal.) *He responded to her clever solution.*
 • (Repeat until firm.)
b. What word refers to solving a problem? (Signal.) *Solution.*
 • What word means **reacted?** (Signal.) *Responded.*
 • What word means **very smart?** (Signal.) *Clever.*

6. Expect student performance to improve **if you bring them to mastery in the early lessons.** You'll find that they tend to learn new sentences with less repetition. You can often provide far less practice and maintain a far less strict criterion of performance. Occasionally, students will need firming, but they will tend to learn the sentences much faster than they do at first.

Word-Attack Exercises

General Information

The words the students are to read during the word-attack portion of the lesson appear in the textbook. The words are in columns, each containing four to seven words.

The main purpose of the word-attack exercises is to teach students the new words that will appear in the stories and information passages they read. For words that students probably understand, there is no work on word meaning. For words that may be unfamiliar to the students, you'll tell the meaning of the word or show how to use the word in a sentence. The words that have a meaning emphasis are scattered throughout the lists. In the sample from lesson 57 (on the next page), there are three words for which you provide information about meaning. (One is in column 2, one is in column 3, and one is in column 4.)

1	2	3
1. demonstrate	1. tremble	1. palms
2. computer	2. cabinet	2. gaining
3. breakfast	3. darkness	3. guests
4. aisle	4. oxygen	4. partly
5. gravity	5. equipment	5. helmets
	6. keyboard	6. provided

4	5
1. survive	1. liquid
2. pressure	2. baggage
3. waist	3. weightless
4. suit	4. fastened

EXERCISE 2
READING WORDS

Column 1

a. **Find lesson 57 in your textbook.** ✓
- Touch column 1. ✓
- (Teacher reference:)

> 1. **demonstrate**   4. **aisle**
> 2. **computer**   5. **gravity**
> 3. **breakfast**

b. Word 1 is **demonstrate.** What word? (Signal.) *Demonstrate.*
c. Word 2 is **computer.** What word? (Signal.) *Computer.*
d. Word 3 is **breakfast.** What word? (Signal.) *Breakfast.*
e. Word 4 is **aisle.** What word? (Signal.) *Aisle.*
f. Word 5. What word? (Signal.) *Gravity.*
g. Let's read those words again.
- Word 1. What word? (Signal.) *Demonstrate.*
- (Repeat for words 2–5.)
h. (Repeat step g until firm.)

Column 2

i. Find column 2. ✓
- (Teacher reference:)

> 1. **tremble**   4. **oxygen**
> 2. **cabinet**   5. **equipment**
> 3. **darkness**   6. **keyboard**

- All these words have more than one syllable. The first part of each word is underlined.
j. Word 1. What's the underlined part? (Signal.) *trem.*
- What's the whole word? (Signal.) *Tremble.*
- Spell **tremble.** Get ready. (Tap for each letter.) *T-R-E-M-B-L-E.*
- Something that trembles shakes a little. What's another way of saying **The building began to shake?** (Signal.) *The building began to tremble.*
k. Word 2. What's the underlined part? (Signal.) *cab.*
- What's the whole word? (Signal.) *Cabinet.*
- Spell **cabinet.** Get ready. (Tap for each letter.) *C-A-B-I-N-E-T.*
l. Word 3. What's the underlined part? (Signal.) *dark.*
- What's the whole word? (Signal.) *Darkness.*
- Spell **darkness.** Get ready. (Tap for each letter.) *D-A-R-K-N-E-S-S.*
m. Word 4. What's the underlined part? (Signal.) *ox.*
- What's the whole word? (Signal.) *Oxygen.*
- Spell **oxygen.** Get ready. (Tap for each letter.) *O-X-Y-G-E-N.*
n. Word 5. What's the underlined part? (Signal.) *equip.*
- What's the whole word? (Signal.) *Equipment.*
o. Word 6. What's the underlined part? (Signal.) *key.*
- What's the whole word? (Signal.) *Keyboard.*
p. Let's read those words again.
- Word 1. What word? (Signal.) *Tremble.*
- (Repeat for words 2–6.)
q. (Repeat step p until firm.)

Column 3

r. Find column 3. ✓
- (Teacher reference:)

1. palms	4. partly
2. gaining	5. helmets
3. guests	6. provided

- All these words have an ending.

s. Word 1. What word? (Signal.) *Palms.*
- The insides of your hands are called palms. Touch the palm of your hand. ✓

t. Word 2. What word? (Signal.) *Gaining.*
- (Repeat for words 3–6.)

u. Let's read those words again.
- Word 1. What word? (Signal.) *Palms.*
- (Repeat for words 2–6.)

v. (Repeat step u until firm.)

Column 4

w. Find column 4. ✓
- (Teacher reference:)

1. survive	3. waist
2. pressure	4. suit

x. Word 1. What word? (Signal.) *Survive.*
- If you survive, you live. If you don't survive, you die. If you live through an earthquake, you survive the earthquake.

y. Word 2. What word? (Signal.) *Pressure.*
- (Repeat for words 3 and 4.)

z. Let's read those words again.
- Word 1. What word? (Signal.) *Survive.*
- (Repeat for words 2–4.)

a. (Repeat step z until firm.)

Column 5

b. Find column 5. ✓
- (Teacher reference:)

1. liquid	3. weightless
2. baggage	4. fastened

c. Word 1. What word? (Signal.) *Liquid.*
- (Repeat for words 2–4.)

d. Let's read those words again.
- Word 1. What word? (Signal.) *Liquid.*
- (Repeat for words 2–4.)

e. (Repeat step d until firm.)

Individual Turns

(For columns 1–5: Call on individual students, each to read one to three words per turn.)

The individual lists have different decoding emphases. In the previous sample, words 1 through 4 in column 1 are difficult to decode. These words are modeled before students read them.

Columns 2 through 5 present decodable words that require no modeling. Column 2 presents multisyllabic words. The first component in each word is underlined. The presentation for these words requires students to attend to the components. (First they read the underlined part of the word; then they read the whole word.) The students also spell some of these words. The words in column 3 have endings. The words in columns 4 and 5 are miscellaneous, decodable words that will appear in the reading selections. For all these words you, (1) indicate the number of the word students are to read; (2) say What word?; (3) then signal. For example, for word 1 you say, Word 1. What word? When you say word 1, students are to touch under the word. When you say, What word? they are to say the word.

The arrangement and focus of the various columns change from one lesson to another. In some lessons, words that have a particular sound feature will be grouped in a column—for instance, words that have the letter combination **ea.** Students spell some words, but never more than four per lesson. Some lists focus on various types of multisyllabic words. Some lists focus on endings. And some lists have no particular focus except that the words will appear in an upcoming reading selection.

The amount of drill and practice that you provide should depend on how well students read selections. If their reading is accurate and fluent (students reading at close to a conversational rate and not generally exceeding the error limit), you can usually go through the word lists very quickly and with very little repetition. If there are some students in the group who are a little weak, give them more individual turns. But do not try to give all students individual turns.

Presenting Word-Attack Exercises

Maintain clear signals. Use a clap or some other *auditory* signal to indicate when the students are to respond. Your signal should follow the last word of the task by one second. The timing should always be the same—very rhythmical and predictable.

Correct signal violations early in the program. If the students do not respond on signal, tell them what they did or what they should do: Wait for the signal, or You're late. Then repeat the task, reinforcing the students if they respond on signal. Once you know that the students are firm, you

can relax the corrections on signal violations, but don't let the students get so sloppy that you can't clearly hear their responses.

Correct droning, sing-song responses. Tell students, Say it the way you talk. Model the correct behavior and enforce it. Also, check your pacing and make sure you model responses in a normal speaking voice.

Confirm all words that are read correctly by the group. This is important early in the program. For example, immediately after the group reads the word **equator,** say, Yes, **equator.** This practice guards against the possibility that some students misread the word but that you didn't hear the misreading.

Correct all word-reading errors immediately. Even if only one student in the group makes an error, say the correct word.

Work within a specified time frame. The word-attack portion of the lesson takes more time on some days than on others. However, even in the longest lessons, *the word-attack portion should not take more than seven or eight minutes.*

Position yourself so you can observe what students are doing. If you are working with a large group of students, do not stand in front of the group as you present the word-attack exercises. Instead, walk among the students. When you stand behind them and look over their shoulders, you can see whether they are pointing to the appropriate words, and you can observe their responses better than if you are in front of them.

A good procedure is to focus on six to eight individual students. Stand behind one of them as you present two or three words. Then move behind another one. Select the students that most probably would make mistakes. Observe whether they are:

- pointing to the appropriate words

- saying the correct words

- initiating the response on signal or waiting for others to lead them

Regular Reading Selections

Reading Mastery Plus Level 4 presents two types of regular reading selections: main stories and comprehension passages. Virtually all regular lessons and checkout lessons have a main story. Not all of these lessons have a comprehension passage. During the first half of the program, a comprehension passage appears in about half of the regular lessons and checkout lessons. In the second half of the program, comprehension passages are less frequent, occurring in less than a quarter of the lessons.

A list of comprehension passages and main stories appears by lesson in Appendix F.

Comprehension Passages

Comprehension passages are designed to prepare students for comprehending details of upcoming main stories. If a story contains information that students probably do not know, a comprehension passage precedes the main story. The comprehension passage is not as long as the main story, usually between 100 and 200 words. For example, a main story may refer to clouds. Before students read this selection, they read a comprehension passage that gives them relevant information about clouds.

If a comprehension passage appears in a lesson, it appears immediately before the reading of the main story. Here's the comprehension passage from lesson 21.

B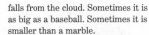

You have read about a big storm cloud. Here are facts about clouds:
- Clouds are made up of tiny drops of water.
- In clouds that are very high, the water drops are frozen. Here is how those clouds look.

Picture 1

- Some kinds of clouds may bring days of bad weather. These are low, flat clouds that look like bumpy blankets.

Picture 2

- Some clouds are storm clouds. They are flat on the bottom, but they go up very high. Sometimes they are five miles high.

Picture 3

The arrows in picture 3 show how the winds move inside a storm cloud. The winds move water drops to the top of the cloud. The drops freeze. When a drop freezes, it becomes a tiny hailstone. The tiny hailstone falls to the bottom of the cloud. At the bottom of the cloud, the tiny hailstone gets covered with more water. Then it goes up again and freezes again. Now the hailstone is a little bigger. It keeps going around and around in the cloud until it gets so heavy that it falls from the cloud. Sometimes it is as big as a baseball. Sometimes it is smaller than a marble.

If you want to see how many times a hailstone has gone to the top of the cloud, break the hailstone in half. You'll see rings. Each ring shows one trip to the top of the cloud. Count the rings and you'll know how many times the hailstone went through the cloud. Hailstone A went through the cloud three times.

How many times did Hailstone B go through the cloud?

Hailstone A

Hailstone B

Main Stories

General Information

For main stories a word-decoding error limit is specified. The error limit for all main stories is based on two errors for each 100 words read aloud. The limits are designed so that students won't become anxious about reading and thus read hesitantly. At the same time, if students perform within the accuracy limits, they are accurately reading 98 out of 100 words.

The procedures for directing the reading of the story are spelled out in detail in the presentation book. Here is the format from lesson 24:

STORY READING

a. Find part C in your textbook. ✓
  - The error limit for group reading is 7 errors. Read carefully.
b. Everybody, touch the title. ✓
  - (Call on a student to read the title.) [Edna Parker.]
  - Everybody, what's the title? (Signal.) Edna Parker.
  - This is the first part of a new story. Everybody, who is this story about? (Signal.) Edna Parker.
  - (Call on individual students to read the story, each student reading two or three sentences at a time. Ask the specified questions as the students read.)

  - (Correct errors: Tell the word. Direct the student to reread the sentence.)
  - (If the group makes more than 7 errors, direct the students to reread the story.)

Edna Parker
Edna Parker was thirteen years old. She had been out on her father's ship before. But this was the first time that her father, Captain Parker, let Edna bring a friend along.

- Everybody, who was Edna Parker's father? (Signal.) *Captain Parker.*
- Had Edna ever been on her father's ship before? (Signal.) *Yes.*
- What was going to be different about this trip? (Call on a student. Idea: *Edna could bring a friend along.*)

This was going to be a great trip for Edna.
On other trips, Edna had a problem. She became bored. There was never anything for her to do on the ship after it left the harbor. Sometimes she would sweep up or help with the meals, but most of the time she just sat around and looked over the side of the ship at the swirling water. With Carla along, Edna would have fun.
. . .

- What was Edna's problem on other trips? (Call on a student. Idea: *She became bored.*)
- What does that mean, she became bored? (Call on a student. Idea: *She didn't have anything to do.*)
- How did Edna usually spend **most** of her time on the ship? (Call on a student. Idea: *Looking over the side of the ship at the swirling water.*)
- What was Edna's friend's name? (Signal.) *Carla.*
- Why would Edna have fun with Carla along? (Call on a student. Idea: *Because she would have someone to do things with.*)
- There are three dots in the story. What does that mean? (Call on a student. Idea: *Part of the story is missing.*)

❁ Captain Parker was explaining the trip to the two girls. He pointed to a map of Florida and the Atlantic Ocean as he spoke.
"We are starting from here," he said, pointing to the tip of Florida. "We are going to follow this dotted line to an island called Andros Island."

- Everybody, touch the part of Florida where the dotted line begins. ✓
- That's where the ship is now. Follow the line to Andros Island. ✓
- That's where they will go. Everybody, tell me the direction they will be going. Get ready. (Signal.) *East.*

Captain Parker continued, "That means we will pass through a place where hundreds of ships have sunk or been lost. It's called the Bermuda Triangle."

- Everybody, what's the name of the dangerous place? (Signal.) *The Bermuda Triangle.*
- What has happened in the Bermuda Triangle? (Call on a student. Idea: *Hundreds of ships have been lost or sunk.*)

Captain Parker continued, "Many sailors say the Bermuda Triangle is the most dangerous part of the ocean."
Carla's face seemed to drop.

- How did Carla feel when her face seemed to drop? (Call on a student. Ideas: *Afraid; surprised; worried.*)
- Everybody, I'll read what Captain Parker said. You make your face drop when you hear the bad news:
    Captain Parker continued, "That means we will pass through a place where hundreds of ships have sunk or been lost. It's called the Bermuda Triangle."
    Captain Parker continued, "Many sailors say the Bermuda Triangle is the most dangerous part of the ocean."

(Students' faces should drop after ". . . the most dangerous part of the ocean.")

"Hey," Captain ⚙ Parker said, and smiled. "Nothing's going to happen in a big ship like this. We are very ⭐ safe. And this is not the stormy season."

- Everybody, did Captain Parker think the trip would be dangerous? (Signal.) *No.*
- He gave two reasons. What were they? (Call on a student. Idea: *The ship was big and it wasn't the stormy season.*)

Carla asked, "Why is the Bermuda Triangle such a dangerous part of the ocean?"
"Bad seas," the captain answered. "There are huge waves and storms that come up without any warning. And there are whirlpools."

- What kinds of things do you find when the seas get bad in the Bermuda Triangle area? (Call on a student. Ideas: *Huge waves; unexpected storms; whirlpools.*)

Edna said, "You know what whirlpools are, don't you, Carla?"
"I think I know what they are," Carla replied.

Captain Parker said, "Let me explain. Did you ever watch water that was going down the drain? Sometimes it spins around and around and it makes the shape of an ice cream cone."
"I've seen those," Carla replied. "They suck water right down the drain."
"Yes," Captain Parker said. "Those are tiny whirlpools. The kind of whirlpools that you find in the Bermuda Triangle are just like those, except they are big enough to suck a ship down."
"Wow," Carla said.

- Read the rest of the story to yourself. Find out three things. Find out how far it is from Florida to Andros Island. Find out how long the trip will take. Find out what the girls should stay away from. Raise your hand when you're finished.

> **Edna was trying to imagine a huge whirlpool.**
>
> **Captain Parker said, "Well, girls, Andros Island is only 120 miles from here, so we should arrive there in less than a day. We should have a smooth trip. The weather looks good. I am going to look over some maps now. You girls may play on deck, but stay away from the sides of the ship. And stay away from the lifeboats."**
>
> **"All right, Dad," Edna said, and the girls rushed onto the deck.**

- (After all students have raised their hand:) Everybody, how far is it from Florida to Andros Island? (Signal.) *120 miles.*
- Everybody, how long will it take the ship to get there? (Signal.) *Less than a day.*
- Name one thing the girls should stay away from. (Call on a student. Ideas: *The sides of the ship; the lifeboats.*)
- Name something else the girls should stay away from. (Call on a student. Ideas: *The lifeboats; the sides of the ship.*)
- I sure hope those girls follow the rules.

- The picture shows Captain Parker's ship. The girls and Captain Parker were in the map room during this story. Everybody, touch the map room. ✓
- At the end of the story, the girls ran out on the deck. Everybody, touch the main deck. ✓
- Touch a lifeboat. ✓

Overview of Story-Reading Procedures

The story-reading procedures change throughout the program. Here is a summary of the procedures.

Lessons 1–12: Students read the **entire** story aloud. You call on individual students, each to read two or three sentences. You present the specified comprehension items.

Lessons 13–140: Students read most of the story aloud. They do not read the last part of the story, however. You present the specified comprehension items. Then students read the end of the story to themselves, and you present comprehension items for that part.

Presenting Reading of Comprehension Passage and Main Story

Here are procedures for effectively directing the group reading of comprehension passages and main stories:

Make sure you receive a good sample of each student's reading behavior. For groups that have over 15 students, you may not receive adequate feedback about the performance of some students. The simplest remedy is to observe students reading individually during paired practice.

Make sure that students follow along as others are reading. Students are to point to the words that are being read. Pointing is a behavioral indication that those students who are not reading aloud are reading silently. Think of the pointing behavior as a way of maximizing practice. By pointing, the students practice reading throughout the group reading. If they don't point, they may practice only when they are reading aloud—a very scant amount of practice.

To ensure that students follow along, establish the procedure that students lose their turn if they don't have their place when they're called on.

If the group is large (over 15), circulate among the students and observe them from behind.

Decoding Errors in Main Stories

Each main story has an error limit. If students are placed appropriately, the group should regularly read within the error limit. Follow these guidelines for dealing with decoding errors:

Remind students of the error limit for the story and tell them how they are doing. Remember, we aren't going to make more than ten errors, so read carefully. Reinforce accurate reading: Good job. You're reading very carefully. Warn the students if they tend to make careless mistakes: The group has already made seven errors, so be careful.

- If the students read within the error limit, congratulate them for doing a good job. Remind them that it is very hard: That was a tough story and this group read it making only __ errors. That's pretty good.

- If the students do not read within the error limit, (1) they are to reread the story, and (2) *you will ask no questions during this rereading.*

Try to schedule the rereading as soon as possible. If there is time in the period, start the rereading immediately. Typically, however, the rereading will have to be scheduled during the next reading lesson.

Tally each error and give immediate feedback. Here is a list of common decoding errors:

- *Omitting an ending.* Saying "look" for *looked* is an error. Saying "run" for *runs* is an error.

- *Saying the wrong word.* Saying "a" for *the* is an error. Saying "what" for *that* is an error.

- *Repeated self-corrections.* A self-correction occurs when a student says the wrong word and then rereads the word correctly before you correct the student. If a student responds with the correct word after some signal has been given that the initial reading was wrong, count the self-correction as an error. If a student does a lot of self-correcting, count all self-corrections as errors. However, if the group makes only occasional self-corrections (no more than 1–3 per story), do not count them as errors.

- *Word omissions or insertions.* If a student reads *They went with the boys from town,* as "They went with the boys from **the** town," count the inserted word as an error. If a student reads the sentence as, "They went with boys from town," the omitted word should be counted as an error.

- *Repeated line skipping.* Like self-corrections, occasional line-skipping should not be treated as an error; simply tell the student to move up to the appropriate line and reread the entire sentence. However, if line-skipping occurs frequently, count each occurrence as one error.

- *Repeated partial readings.* If a student usually reads sentences in this manner: "They went with went with the boys from town," count one error. Occasional rereadings to fix the phrasing of the sentence are acceptable. Chronic rereadings, however, should be treated as errors.

- *Repeated word-part or syllable reading.* If a student usually pronounces longer words a part at a time before saying the word, the student is making decoding errors. Count each **chronic** occurrence of word-part or syllable reading as one error. For example, if the student reads "Ma—manu—manufac—manufacture," count one error.

Remember, the number of decoding errors will drop if you:

- give the students feedback on how they are doing.

- make sure that you are not letting errors pass.

- respond immediately to mistakes.

Correcting Decoding Errors During Selection Reading

There is only one procedure for correcting decoding errors during selection reading:

1. Stop the reader as soon as you hear the error.

2. Indicate whether the reader skipped a line, reread a word, omitted a word, or misread a word. For misread words, say the word and ask the student to repeat it: That word is _____. What word?

3. Direct the student to read the sentence from the beginning: Go back to the beginning of that sentence and read it again.

The last step is particularly important. The only way you know whether the correction was effectively communicated is that the student correctly reads the sentence in which the mistake occurred.

Recording Performance

The reproducible group summary chart that appears in Appendix H is designed for keeping track of:

- the group's performance on the reading of the main story;

- the performance of individual students on their five-lesson reading checkouts;

- students' tenth-lesson test performance;

- students' independent work.

Each chart covers a ten-lesson span. The sample chart on the next page has been partially filled in for lessons 41 to 50.

Teacher **Ms. Turner** Reading Mastery Plus Level 4 Group **2**

Lessons	4 1	4 2	4 3	4 4	CO 4 5	4 6	4 7	4 8	4 9	CO/Test 5	
Main Story Errors	11	12	10	12	(16)	11	10	14	12		
Name	IW	IW	IW	IW	CO	IW	IW	IW	IW	IW	CO	Test
Luis Cepeda												
Yoko Higashi												
Anita Diaz												
Denise Barton												
Zachary Gray												
Eric Adler												

The top of the chart provides the summary information for the group. You record the number of errors the group made in reading each main story. If the group exceeds the error limit, you circle the number. The 16 for lesson 45 is circled because the error limit for lesson 45 is 15.

Presenting Comprehension Activities

The presentation script for each main story and comprehension passage indicates the comprehension items you are to present.

Present items specified during the reading. Comprehension passages and main stories are read once. The text indicates both the items that are to be presented and when they are to be presented.

The teacher presentation book shows the material that the students are reading.

Excerpts from the student text appear in boldface type that is over a screen.

The following sample is from lesson 29. The boldface text in the screened boxes is the story the students read. The items below the boxes refer to the text immediately above them. The students read, "The size of the footprints told Edna something about the size of the animal." You say, What would you know about the size of an animal that had footprints a yard long?

For some illustrations, the illustrations are reproduced in the script, and items immediately follow the illustration. In the sample, the script shows an illustration followed by the item, Everybody, touch the groove in the picture.

STORY READING

a. Find part B in your textbook. ✓
- The error limit for group reading is 12 errors. Read carefully.

b. Everybody, touch the title. ✓
- (Call on a student to read the title.) *[Footprints.]*
- Everybody, what's the title? (Signal.) *Footprints.*
- (Call on individual students to read the story, each student reading two or three sentences at a time. Ask the specified questions as the students read.)

> - (Correct errors: Tell the word. Direct the student to reread the sentence.)
> - (If the group makes more than 12 errors, direct the students to reread the story.)

Footprints

There was a row of footprints in the red sand. The footprints of the animal were a yard long. Each footprint had three toes. The size of the footprints told Edna something about the size of the animal.

- What would you know about the size of an animal that had footprints a yard long? (Call on a student. Idea: *It would be a big animal.*)

The footprints made very deep dents in the sand. These deep dents told Edna something about how much the animal weighed.

- What could the deep dents tell you? (Call on a student. Idea: *The animal weighed a lot.*)
- Everybody, which would make deeper dents, an animal that weighed **one hundred** pounds or an animal that weighed **one thousand** pounds? (Signal.) *An animal that weighed one thousand pounds.*

Between the footprints was a deep groove in the sand. Carla asked, "What could make that deep trail?"

- Everybody, touch the groove in the picture. ✓
- The groove goes where the footprints go. What could make that deep groove? (Call on individual students. Ideas: *A branch the animal was dragging; a tail;* etc.)
- Let's find out what made it.

Suddenly Edna shouted, "A tail. I'll bet a tail did that. That animal is walking on its hind legs. It's dragging a heavy tail behind it. The tail makes the groove in the sand."

For a while, the girls walked around the footprints and didn't say anything. Then they looked toward the jungle. The animal had left a huge path through the jungle. On either side of this path were thick vines and trees. But the path was almost clear. It looked as if somebody had driven a truck through the jungle and knocked down all the small trees and vines.

- Everybody, touch the path that goes into the jungle in the picture on page 143. ✓
- Can you see any trees that were knocked over when that animal went through the jungle? (Signal.) *Yes.*

⚙ Edna said, "I don't think we should go into that jungle."

"Yeah, we shouldn't do it," Carla said. The girls were silent for a few moments. They just stood there and looked at the great path that led into the jungle. Then Carla said, "But we could follow that path for a little way. We don't have to go too far."

- Do you think they'll follow that path? (Call on individual students. Student preference.)

"I don't want to go in there," Edna said. But she wasn't telling Carla the truth. Part of her was frightened and wanted to run away. But part of her wanted to see what made those huge footprints. Her mind made pictures of that animal. In one of the pictures, the animal was chasing 🌸 Carla and Edna. Edna was running as fast as she could, but the animal was getting closer and closer and . . .

- Edna stopped right in the middle of this thought. Let's find out why.

"Come on," Carla said. "Let's go just a little way."

- Why did Edna stop imagining what the animal was like? (Call on a student. Idea: *Carla started talking.*)

Now another part of Edna's mind was taking over. It wanted to see that animal. This part of Edna's mind was not terribly frightened. It made up pictures of Carla and Edna sneaking up on the animal. In these pictures, the animal did not see Edna 🌟 and Carla. "This animal is not very smart," Edna said to herself. "If it was a smart animal, it would have found us last night. Maybe it does not have a good sense of smell. Maybe it has poor eyes."

- Why didn't Edna think the animal was very smart? (Call on a student. Idea: *Because it didn't find them last night.*)
- What two things did Edna think might be wrong with the animal? (Call on a student. Idea: *It might have poor eyesight or a poor sense of smell.*)
- She thought the animal might have poor eyes. What does that mean? (Call on a student. Idea: *It could not see very well.*)

"Okay, let's follow the path," Edna said to Carla. "But just a little way."
Carla picked up a short, heavy branch. She practiced swinging it like a club. Edna picked up a branch too.

They were easy to find in the path made by the animal.

- Why were they easy to find? (Call on a student. Idea: *The animal knocked branches off the trees.*)
- What do you think they planned to do with the clubs? (Call on a student. Idea: *Protect themselves.*)

So the girls started down the path into the jungle. They walked very slowly and carefully. They jumped each time a screech or a roar came from the jungle. They tried not to step on small branches that would make a cracking sound.

- Why? (Call on a student. Idea: *So the animal wouldn't hear them.*)

Slowly, they moved farther into the jungle. Soon, Edna could not see the beach behind her. The trees over them blocked out the light.
"This is far enough," Edna said after she realized that the girls had gone over a hundred meters into the jungle.
"Shhh," Carla said, and pointed straight ahead. Edna could see a clearing. In the middle of it was a small pond. From the pond, steam rose into the air. The girls moved forward. Now Edna could see a small stream flowing into the pond. And she saw tall grass.

- What things did Edna see in the clearing? (Call on a student. Ideas: *A pond with steam rising from it; a stream; tall grass.*)
- The picture shows the clearing. There are no trees in the clearing. Everybody, touch the pond. ✓
- Touch the steam that is rising into the air. ✓
- Touch the stream. ✓
- Touch the tall grass. ✓
- Read the rest of the story to yourself. I'm not going to tell you things to read for. So read it very carefully and be ready to answer some questions. Raise your hand when you're finished.

> **When the girls reached the edge of the clearing, Edna stopped. She noticed that the trees were very strange. She looked at a small tree on the edge of the clearing. "I saw a picture of a tree like this somewhere," she said. "But I can't remember where." She tried to remember. Suddenly, she did. And when she remembered, she wanted to run from the jungle as fast as she could. She had seen a picture of that tree in a book on dinosaurs. She had looked at the picture in the book many times. And she clearly remembered the tree. It was in a picture that showed Tyrannosaurus fighting with Triceratops.**
>
> **Edna looked at the tree and remembered the huge footprints. "Oh no," she said aloud.**

- (After all students have raised their hand:) Edna saw something next to the path that she recognized from a picture in a book. Everybody, what was that? (Signal.) *A tree.*
- What else was in the picture that showed the tree? (Call on a student. Ideas: *Dinosaurs; Tyrannosaurus fighting with Triceratops.*)

- When Edna remembered the picture, she thought of the footprints on the beach. Then she said, "Oh no," aloud. She had figured out something. What was that? (Call on a student. Idea: *Dinosaurs were on the island.*)

Do not become sidetracked into long discussions. Certainly you may present additional tasks; however, these should be infrequent. For example, if the students have had problems with a particular name or concept, it's all right to add a task even though the script does not indicate an item. If a specified task asks for student opinions, do not poll the entire group. A couple of quick responses will suffice.

Use the wording indicated in the script. Tasks that begin with the word *everybody* call for a group, unison response. Tasks that say *Call on a student* are to be presented to a single student. Tasks that are followed by *Call on individual students* call for a range of responses. In some cases, the task will call for an opinion, such as: What do you think will happen? In other cases, the students are asked to name items that fall into a particular category: Name some animals that are warm-blooded.

Accept appropriate ideas for tasks that are answered by an individual. The appropriate response for the second task in the sample (What could the deep dents tell you?) is expressed as an idea. (Idea: *The animal weighed a lot.*) An appropriate response is one that clearly expresses this **idea,** regardless of the specific words used in the response—*it was heavy.* Present a follow-up task if the response is not sufficiently specific. For example, if a student responds "how much it weighs," you would say, If an animal made deep dents, would it weigh **a lot** or **not very much?**

Reducing Comprehension Errors

If the students make a mistake on an oral comprehension task, correct the error, mark the task, and tell them: I'm going to ask that question later. So remember the answer. At the end of the story, present any marked tasks. If an individual turn was missed, present the task to an individual (not necessarily the same one who missed the task).

Correcting Comprehension Errors During Selection Reading

You will correct two types of tasks: tasks in which students have just read the passage that answers the questions and tasks in which the information was presented earlier.

For each type of correction, you will follow this general pattern:

1. Make sure students have the information they need to answer the question.

2. Repeat the task.

3. Repeat the task again at a later time.

For different item types, there are corresponding variations of this correction.

- If the passage the students just read answers the question, reread the passage or summarize the content before repeating the task the students missed.

- If the passage students just read does not answer the question, you will tell the students the information they need to answer the question before you repeat the task.

- If the passage does not give the answer and if further facts will not clarify the answer, you tell them the answer, then repeat the task.

When information is presented in the passage students just read, you make sure they have the information they need either by rereading the passage or by telling them the relevant information. Sometimes, you'll be able to give them the information they need by asking them a series of questions. If you can't think of good questions to ask, however, you can simply tell them the information they need.

Example: Why didn't Edna think the animal was very smart? A student responds, *"He has a small brain."*

1. **Repeat the part that answers the question:** Listen to that part again: "This animal is not very smart," Edna said to herself. "If it was a smart animal, it would have found us last night."

2. **Repeat the task:** Why didn't Edna think the animal was very smart?

3. **Give the correct answer, if necessary:** If the student doesn't respond appropriately, say, It would have found them the night before.

4. **Remind the students that you'll repeat the task at a later time:** Remember that answer. I'm going to ask the question later. At a later time, repeat the question.

When not all information is presented in the passage students just read, you provide students with the information they need.

Here's the correction for a mistake from lesson 29.

Example: What would you know about the size of an animal that had footprints a yard long?

1. **Present an easier version of the question:** What kind of animal would have footprints a yard long, a big animal or a small animal?

2. **Repeat the task:** What would you know about the size of an animal that had footprints a yard long?

3. **Give the correct answer, if necessary:** It's a really big animal.

4. **Repeat the task at a later time.**

At the end of the period, or at another time the group members are present (after recess, just before lunch, etc.) ask the students questions they missed. Remember to give them enough story information for them to answer the question.

When additional facts do not clarify the answer:

1. **Tell students the answer.**

2. **Repeat the task.**

3. **Repeat the task at a later time.**

Note that these items usually ask "Why?" or require students to make a judgment or draw a conclusion. Here's another example from lesson 29: Why were they (branches) easy to find? A student responds, "*I don't know.*"

Here's the correction:

1. **Tell the student the answer:** Because the animal had knocked branches off the trees.

2. **Repeat the original task:** Why were they easy to find?

3. **Remind the students that you'll repeat the task at a later time.**

Correcting Errors on Picture Tasks

Some picture tasks require students to touch an illustration or operate on it in some way. The task may be, Touch that path, or Touch the steam rising from the pond. These tasks are presented to the group, but are not accompanied by a signal to respond. Responses are incorrect if students:

• copy responses produced by a neighbor

• touch the wrong object

• fail to respond

• give ambiguous responses

To correct picture mistakes, show the students the right response. If possible, repeat the task later.

Example: The picture (seen on the next page) shows geese flying in a V, with dark blue air showing air that's standing still and light blue air showing air that's moving in the same direction as the flock. The task is: Hold your finger on your book and point to show the direction the light blue air is moving. The mistake: A student points in a vague manner above the page. The correction: Put your finger right on the page. Now point to show the direction the light blue air is moving. Do not accept ambiguous responses.

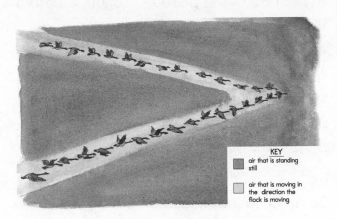

KEY

☐ air that is standing still

☐ air that is moving in the direction the flock is moving

Some picture tasks require students to observe details of pictures and produce **verbal** responses about these details. Treat these verbal responses the same way you would treat responses to a written question. The picture answers the question you ask, so you would tell students the answer, repeat the task, and possibly repeat it later (although it may be difficult to do this without the book).

Here's an example from lesson 78.

What kind of animal is at the top of the pyramid? *Parrot.*

Correction:

1. **You tell the answer:** It's a pigeon.

2. **You repeat the task:** What kind of animal is at the top of the pyramid?

3. **Later you can ask students a question that is like the one you presented.**

Paired Practice

General Information

Following the main-story reading, students work in pairs and reread the story with each student reading half of the story. Students are permanently assigned. Partners are to sit next to each other. They can either read from the same text or from two texts. Allow 10 to 12 minutes for paired practice.

Possible Problems

Here are the more common problems teachers encounter when implementing paired-practice procedures:

1. Students take too long to get started.

2. Students take too long to complete the reading.

3. Students become lax about following along when they are not reading and therefore do not respond to the partner's errors.

For problem 1: The simplest way to get students into reading faster is to have a structured beginning. One good plan is to require some sort of response for the pair—such as both partners sitting next to each other with books in place and raising their hands. They are not to start reading until you acknowledge that they have raised their hands.

It's time for paired practice. Raise your hand when you and your partner are ready.

Acknowledge each pair and tell them to start.

Praise students who start quickly, That was a good start. Almost all the teams are ready to read.

If some partners consistently take more than a few seconds to get ready for the paired practice, reassign the members of the team, or place a stronger contingency on getting started on time.

For problem 2: Set up a reinforcing contingency for completing the reading in a reasonable amount of time. If students often take 15 minutes to complete the reading, set the time limit at 14 minutes and give students who perform within this time limit praise and possibly some other reinforcer. After students consistently read within 14 minutes, change the time limit to 13 minutes, and so on.

For problem 3: Monitor the students as they read and have students report on their partner's errors.

If students are not catching errors their partners make, require the checker to write the number of errors the partner made.

At the end of the paired practice, record a quick summary:

A team, raise your hand if your partner made no errors.

Raise your hand if your partner made 1 or 2 errors.

Raise your hand if your partner made more than two errors.

Summarize the results on the board. Then conclude, Well, it looks like the B team won today, but not by much. We'll see who wins next time.

The system works because the students want their team to win. If students miss their partner's errors, however, the partner's team gets an advantage.

Independent Work

General Information

As part of every lesson, the students work independently for about 20 to 30 minutes, completing all the textbook items specified for that lesson as well as completing side 1 and side 2 of that lesson's worksheet.

Here are the types of items students work:

- Items based on the comprehension passage read that day (only on lessons that have a comprehension passage);

- Items based on the main story in the lesson;

- Skill items (sequencing, vocabulary review, crossword puzzles, etc.);

- Review items based on information from earlier lessons (either from comprehension passages or main stories).

Early Preparation

During the first part of the program, the teacher reads the items.

- Lessons 1–3. The teacher reads all independent work items aloud. After reading each item, the teacher calls on a student to answer the item. The teacher corrects mistakes and repeats items that students miss.

- Lessons 4–5. After the main story, individual students orally read and answer the items for the comprehension passage and the main story. The teacher reads review items and introduces new types of skill items.

- Lessons 6–9. After the main story, individual students orally read and answer the items for the comprehension passage and the main story.

- Lessons 11–14. After the main story, students orally read the items for the comprehension passage and main story. The teacher continues to introduce new types of skill items.

- Lessons 15–16. After the main story, students orally read only the main story items. The teacher continues to introduce new types of skill items.

- Lessons 17–140. As a rule some items appear in the textbook and some on the worksheets. The teacher does not read items, with the exception of specific skill items.

When new types of skill items are introduced, the teacher goes over them with the students.

Observe Students as They Work Independently

Plan to observe the group at work on the independent-work activities every few lessons, especially during the first 20 lessons.

Identify specific problems students have. Make sure they are on task and are not copying from each other. Serious problems should be corrected immediately.

Is the student reading items correctly? As part of answering correctly, students must read items correctly. Often it is possible to infer how a student misread an item from the response. For example, an item reads, "Why did Edna stop imagining what the animal was like?" The student answers, "Yes." Inference: The student read the item as "Did Edna stop imagining what the animal was like?" Tell the student: I don't think you read that item carefully. Read it again.

Note: As a rule, you shouldn't help a student more than once during a lesson. The more you help, the less information you have about what a student actually knows, and the more the student will rely on you for help.

Is the student working at a reasonable rate? Students who are just learning how to work independently often don't use their time well. They need feedback about how much time has passed and how they are performing.

A good tactic is to remind the students about their rate of performance. As you observe individual students, make positive comments to the group about individual students' rates: Oh, here's somebody who's already finished the workbook items. Very good . . . Here's somebody else who is almost that far along. Fantastic.

If the students tend to go slowly, make sure you give students feedback about how they are doing as they work. For example, after they have worked for about fifteen minutes, remind them that they should have finished about half the independent work assignment.

Help students who get "stuck" on a particular item. They may not have a strategy for completing the exercises and then returning to problem items. Explain the strategy of (1) circling the number of a problem item, (2) skipping that item and working all non-problem items, and (3) returning to the problem (circled) item.

Are the answers to items correct? Refer to the answer key. If the answer a student wrote is not correct, tell the student something like: Your answer to item 5 is not correct. You should not tell the student the answer, and usually you should not provide more than one of these prompts to each student per lesson.

Answers that are obviously correct present no problem. But you may have questions about answers that have grammatical errors, that do not correspond precisely to the answer given in the answer key, or that contain misspelled words.

Some of the answers in the key are labeled "Idea." This designation means that the student's response must give a correct answer; however, the students are not required to use the exact words that appear in the key. The reason these items are shown as having "idea" answers is that there are different ways of expressing the answer, and all answers that express the idea are equally correct.

Here's an item with some responses that students wrote. Item: Why wouldn't Edna be bored on this trip?

In the selection, Edna's friend Carla is coming on the trip with her.

Below is the answer key for this item:

3. Why wouldn't Edna be bored on this trip?
Idea: Her friend Carla was along.

Below are responses students wrote. Some of these answers are clearly correct or incorrect. Others present problems. You can test the items by asking yourself, Do I know what the student is trying to say? Did the student use enough words to really say that? Can I overlook any wording misuse and still judge that the student expressed the idea?

1. *Because Carla wouldn't make her boring.* Clearly, the student means that Carla's presence would keep Edna's trip from being boring. The answer probably expresses the right idea.

2. *She'd play with her friend.* This answer has no problems. It clearly expresses the idea and uses adequate wording.

3. *Her friend.* The answer is wrong. It does not answer the question: Why wouldn't Edna be bored on this trip?

4. *She'd play.* The answer is clearly wrong. She could play on any of the trips; what's different about this trip is that she'll have someone to play with.

5. *Carla.* The answer may be correct but like some of the others above, it is incomplete. Something about Carla prevented the trip from being boring. (Carla was with Edna.)

6. *She was there.* The answer is clearly wrong. To be correct, it would have to say something like, "They were there." In other words, they were together. With no more information than "she was there," however, we don't know who the *she* was or if there was more than one *she*.

7. *It was a long trip.* The answer is clearly wrong. The trip is the same length whether or not Carla is there. The trip would seem longer if Carla was not there, because it would be boring. But that idea is not implied by the student's response.

Do students spell the words correctly? Here are some rules about spelling errors for **words that are not spelling words:**

1. If the word appears in the item, it should be spelled correctly in the answer.

2. If the word does not appear in the item, it will not be counted wrong if it is spelled incorrectly.

If *earthquake* is a spelling word, the students could be held accountable for it.

However, don't try to identify every spelling word students should know. Spot-check items as you monitor the students. If you notice spelling words that are misspelled, mark them, but focus primarily on the words in the item. If the answers have words that appear in the item, the words should be spelled correctly.

Are the answers to *how* and *why* questions expressed appropriately? Some students do not write appropriate answers to these questions. For instance, the item, "Why did he go to the library?" is appropriately answered, "To get a book," or "Because he wanted a book," or "He wanted a book." Some students, however, may write, "A book." That answer is unacceptable.

To correct this type of response, present items orally. Then direct students to write appropriate answers.

Note that when students answer the questions orally, they tend to answer them correctly. For example:

Listen: Why did he go to the library?

To get a book.

Yes, **to get a book.** Those are the words that answer the question. Say those words.

To get a book.

Write them.

Present tasks like the previous one until students are very firm on the words they are to write.

Remedies for students who can't remember story information. Starting with lesson 17 the basic procedure is for students to complete their independent work without first hearing items read or answered. Students are supposed to remember the information from reading the story and answering the oral comprehension items (which usually include all the written items they will respond to).

If some students have great difficulty remembering the information from the story and continue to make mistakes on independent work because they don't recall the answers, you may introduce a temporary procedure:

- Direct students who have problems remembering the information to write answers to all the items they can work.

- Next, have them circle the number of any items they cannot answer.

- Direct them to read these items to themselves.

- Tell them, Remember the questions that are circled because you'll look in your story to find the answers.

- Permit them to look at their story one time to find answers to all items. Students are not to write anything during the time they are looking in the story. Also, students are to limit their information search to the lesson that was read today. They are not to refer to earlier selections.

  Pencils down. You may look at today's story one time to find answers you couldn't remember. You have three minutes. You have to find

answers to all your questions in three minutes. You can't write anything until you're done reading.

- Monitor students and make sure that they do not write the answer to one question and then attempt to look at the story again. Remind them, You can only look at the story one time.

Repeat the procedure on no more than 12 lessons. Remind students that they should try to remember the answers when the story is being read by the group. Reinforce students who improve in remembering information.

Workchecks

General Information

The goal of the workcheck is to review the independent-work tasks and to make sure that (1) students are not making too many errors and (2) students learn the correct answers to items they miss. The workcheck is not mere paper marking. It is teaching. It is particularly important for *Reading Mastery Plus* Level 4 because many items will appear as review items on later lessons. Some students will miss these items repeatedly unless you present daily workchecks.

The independent work consists of the worksheet pages for the lesson and answers to textbook items written on lined paper.

During the workcheck, you go over all the items and students mark all items that are wrong.

At the end of the workcheck students record the total number of errors they made at the top of the lined paper. Students change all incorrect answers and hand in their lined paper and their worksheet (side 1 and side 2).

You quickly spot-check the worksheet answers and those on lined paper. Don't spot-check only items that had mistakes, because some students are not reliable about marking incorrect answers.

After the spot-check, you will use the Group Summary Chart to record the number of errors each student made on the lesson. (See **Recording Errors,** page 57.)

A "passing grade" for each lesson is three or fewer errors. This criterion is fairly stiff because many lessons call for 35–40 responses. The structure of the program makes it possible for most students to pass almost all lessons. The record of errors may be used to award grades. More importantly, the error performance indicates how well the students are performing, what they are mastering, and whether they need additional practice.

The workchecks are designed to provide that practice and to assure that students continue to perform well in the lessons.

A workcheck is most efficiently handled as a group activity. It should be conducted some time after the group has completed the independent work activities, but before the next lesson is presented.

Although details of the procedure may vary from situation to situation, here are things you should do during the daily workcheck:

- Check the written responses to all items. (Answer keys for worksheet and textbook items appear in the Answer Key book.)

- Make sure that all incorrect responses are marked with an **X.**

- Give the students information about correct answers to items, so they can later change their incorrect answers.

- Make a final check of each student's written work after the student has changed all the incorrect answers.

- Then record the number of errors (the number of items originally marked with an X and later corrected).

The workcheck should not take a great deal of time. In most cases, it requires only six to nine minutes. If it takes much longer, (a) your pacing is too slow, or (b) the students are not firm in some skills that are important in completing the independent work. Work on both possibilities.

Presenting Workchecks

Students may check their own independent work during the workcheck. They should use a colored pencil for checking.

The fastest procedure for going through the workcheck is for you to **read each item and call on a student to tell the correct answer.** Students who have questions may raise their hand. If many students have questions about a particular item, tell them to mark the item with a question mark. Go quickly to the next item.

As you read the items and give the answers, circulate among the students. Make sure they are marking each incorrect response with an **X.** By circulating among the students, you will discourage the students' tendency to change their answers without first marking the item as incorrect.

Firm items that a lot of students tend to miss, and firm students who consistently make more than three errors on their independent work. You firm by giving additional practice.

There are different formats for firming, but the simplest is for you to go over the items that many students miss and provide paired practice for students who tend to make too many errors.

Don't try to firm all difficult items during one session. Instead, give students short bursts of practice (10–15 trials) in possibly three or four lessons.

For students who consistently make three or more errors, provide paired practice. Pair the lower students with students who do well on the independent work. The higher student presents the various items the other student missed and gives feedback on each answer. The paired practice could be scheduled for about five minutes a lesson (possibly at the end of the workcheck period).

Plan to firm students on sets of related facts. For example, some students have trouble with facts that present numbers—what's the speed of sound, what's the speed of light, how long does it take Io to go around Jupiter, how far is it from the sun to the earth, how long does it take light to travel from the sun to the earth,

how long does it take Jupiter to spin around one time.

If students tend to confuse the numbers or just can't remember them, plan to provide a short review at the end of each lesson, until the students perform well. The review should not last more than 2 minutes and should not have more than three unfamiliar or unfirm facts. There's no problem if the review contains facts that are firm. For instance, if students know two of the facts above and are weak on the remaining four, present a group of items that consists of the two firm facts and three of the facts that are not firm. If students perform well, present the full set of six facts on the next lesson. Continue presenting this set on the following lessons (with the items in different orders) until students are firm on all items. This is a variation of the fact-review format, with specifically selected items. A sample of a fact review appears below.

EXERCISE 3

FACT REVIEW

a. Let's review some facts you have learned. First we'll go over the facts together. Then I'll call on some of you to do some facts.

b. Everybody, name the ocean the Bermuda Islands are in. (Pause.) Get ready. (Signal.) *Atlantic Ocean.*
- Name the ocean you go through when you go **west** from the United States. (Pause.) Get ready. (Signal.) *Pacific Ocean.*
- Tell me if things look **light** or **dark** when you're scuba diving 100 feet deep. (Pause.) Get ready. (Signal.) *Dark.*
- (Repeat step b until firm.)

c. Let's say you open a bottle of soda pop. Tell me if the pressure inside the bottle goes **up** or **down**. (Pause.) Get ready. (Signal.) *Down.*
 • Tell me what forms in the soda pop. (Pause.) Get ready. (Signal.) *Bubbles.*
 • Name the arrow-shaped fish that live in the ocean. (Pause.) Get ready. (Signal.) *Barracudas.*
 • (Repeat step c until firm.)

d. Tell me if the water in the ocean is warmer **at 100 feet down** or **at the surface.** (Pause.) Get ready. (Signal.) *At the surface.*
 • Tell me if all the water at 100 feet down is the same temperature. (Pause.) Get ready. (Signal.) *No.*
 • Tell me what a buoyancy device is filled with. (Pause.) Get ready. (Signal.) *Air.*
 • (Repeat step d until firm.)

Individual Turns

Now I'm going to call on individual students to do some facts. (Call on individual students to do the set of facts in step b, step c, or step d.)

The review consists of three or four items that students tend to confuse and two or three items that generally give students no trouble. You may use this format for any group of items that students tend to confuse.

If students make a lot of mistakes on independent work, direct them to redo either the entire page on which the errors occurred, or just the part that presented problems.

Recording Errors

Record errors for independent work for the students *after* you have looked at their corrected work. The number of independent-work errors has been written by the students at the top of the lined paper (at the end of the workcheck). Check the numbers for accuracy. Record

the number of errors in column **IW** of your Group Summary Chart.

The sample Group Summary Chart on the next page has been filled out for lessons 41 through 49. The shaded areas show the parts of the chart used for recording independent-work errors.

A passing grade for each lesson is three or fewer errors. Yoko Higashi's **IW** performance for lesson 41 is circled, indicating that a remedy is needed.

It is important to monitor students' independent work performance. If students start making a large number of errors on their independent work, firm them before proceeding in the program.

Individual Reading Checkouts

General Information

During every fifth lesson, starting with lesson 10, each student receives an individual reading checkout. In these lessons that end with the digit 5 (15, 25, etc.), the paired practice is deleted. Students therefore have time for the individual checkouts. The average time available for individual reading checkouts is about fifteen minutes.

Checkouts take about a minute-and-a-half per student. If the group is large, you may need an additional checker. You may use an aide, an older student, a parent volunteer, or possibly a higher-performing student in the classroom. The main qualification for a checker is the ability to identify reading errors and keep accurate time. If an additional checker is not available, you may be able to finish the

GROUP SUMMARY CHART
Reading Mastery Plus
Level 3

Teacher **Ms. Turner** Group **2**

Lessons	4 1	4 2	4 3	4 4	CO 4 5		4 6	4 7	4 8	4 9	CO/Test 5	
Main Story Errors	7	8	8	8		(9)	11	7	5	9		
Name	IW	IW	IW	IW	CO	IW	IW	IW	IW	IW	CO	Test
Luis Cepeda	2	1	2	1	/	2	1	0	1	3	/	
Yoko Higashi	(4)	3	2	2	/	2	3	1	2	2	/	
Anita Diaz	1	1	1	0	/	2	1	1	0	2	/	
Denise Barton	1	2	0	1	/	1	0	1	0	2	/	
Zachary Gray	1	0	0	1	/	1	2	1	1	1	/	
Eric Adler	2	1	1	0	/	1	0	1	0	2	/	
					/						/	

checkouts at some later time in the school day. Possibly, you could finish them during the next lesson.

Each checkout is conducted by an aide, adult volunteer, or by the teacher.

To conduct checkouts, the checker calls up individual students as the group works on independent-work activities. The student orally reads a specified passage from the main story of the preceding lesson. For example, for the checkout in lesson 30, each student reads a specified passage from lesson 29. The passage in the student textbook has marks at the beginning and at the end (✿).

The checker times each student. **To pass the checkout, the student must read the passage in one minute or less and make no more than two errors.**

Conducting Individual Reading Checkouts

Identify a part of the room where a student can read individually to you or to the assigned checker. The simplest procedure is for the checker to:

• Sit next to the student.

• Tell the student when to begin reading.

• Observe the text that the student reads.

• Make a tally mark on a sheet of paper for each error.

• Help if the student gets stuck on a word for more than two seconds.

• Record the time it takes the student to complete the passage.

Decoding errors consist of word misidentifications, word omissions, line-skipping, and word additions. (Self-corrects and rereading words also may be counted as errors. See pages 41 and 42.)

Note that the checker is not to correct errors unless the correction is necessary for the student to keep reading the passage. If the student can't read a word within about two seconds, the checker says the word and marks it as an error. The checker may first ask, "Do you want me to tell you the word?"

Students' Records

Each student keeps a record of reading checkout performance with thermometer charts (reproducible copies of which are at the back of student workbooks and in Appendix J of this guide). During the program, the student will fill in two thermometer charts. Together, they show all the reading checkouts the student passed.

- The current thermometer charts may be posted in the classroom, kept in individual student folders, or in a central folder that you keep.

- If a student passes a checkout on the first trial, the student colors the appropriate space of the thermometer red. For example, if the student passes the checkout for lesson 35, the student colors the space for 35 red.

- If the student passes the checkout, but not on the first trial, the student colors the appropriate space, but not red. You may use blue, black, pink, or some other color.

When the student completes *Reading Mastery Plus* Level 4, both thermometer charts should be completely filled in. The colors show whether the student needed additional firming, and where that firming occurred.

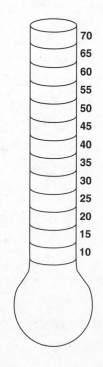

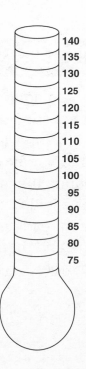

Recording Rate-and-Accuracy Performance

Use column **CO** on the Group Summary Chart to record the number of errors each student made and whether the student passed (**P**) or failed (**F**) the rate criterion (one minute or less).

The **CO** columns on the Group Summary Chart have two parts. Record **P** or **F** in the top half of the box to indicate whether the student **passed** or **failed** the rate criterion. Record the student's number of decoding errors in the bottom half of the box.

The sample Group Summary Chart on page 61 has been filled out for lessons 41 through 50. The shaded columns show the parts of the chart used to record rate and accuracy performance for the individual reading checkouts in lesson 45 and lesson 50 (test 5). Note that Denise Barton's **CO** performance for lesson 45 is circled, indicating that a remedy is needed.

Firming Students Who Do Not Pass Checkouts

The students who do not pass a checkout on their first attempt should reread the passage aloud to their partner until they achieve an acceptable rate-accuracy performance. During these readings, students should be told which words they missed. After each reading, they should study the passage and then reread that passage to the partner.

Students who don't pass two consecutive attempts to meet the rate-accuracy criterion for a checkout should receive additional oral-reading practice.

- This practice should be modeled after the individual reading checkouts, with the exception that the student who is reading should receive immediate feedback about words that are misread. The checker simply tells the correct word.

- A plan that works well is to direct the student to read the last two or three stories that the group has read. Use the same error limit that is specified for group reading.

- Monitor the student's paired-reading practice. Make sure that the student is participating and the partner is responding to any mistakes the reader makes. If the practice is not adequate, either reassign the student to another partner or increase the amount of paired-reading practice the student receives.

Often, the student who is weak in decoding will tend to make a greater number of errors when tackling long passages. Therefore, the checker can take turns with the student, the checker reading one paragraph (or a few lines) and the student reading the next few lines.

A good variation is for the checker to read somewhat haltingly and make mistakes from time to time. The student is to catch these mistakes. By reading haltingly, the checker ensures that the student will be able to follow along. Requiring the student to catch the checker's mistakes ensures that the student is attending to

Teacher __Ms. Turner__   Reading Mastery Plus Level 4   Group __2__

Lessons	41	42	43	44	CO 45	45	46	47	48	49	CO/Test 5	
Main Story Errors	11	12	10	12	(16)		11	10	14	12		
Name	IW	IW	IW	IW	CO	IW	IW	IW	IW	IW	CO	Test
Luis Cepeda	2	1	2	1	P/0	2	1	0	1	3	P/0	
Yoko Higashi	(4)	3	2	2	P/0	2	3	1	2	2	P/1	
Anita Diaz	1	1	1	0	P/0	2	1	1	0	2	P/0	
Denise Barton	1	2	0	1	F/1	1	0	1	0	2	P/2	
Zachary Gray	1	0	0	1	P/0	1	2	1	1	1	P/0	
Eric Adler	2	1	1	0	P/1	1	0	1	0	2	P/1	

the words even when not reading aloud. The periods during which the checker reads are therefore not merely "breaks." They are a switch from one kind of accuracy performance to another.

Fact Games

General Information

Fact games occur every tenth lesson as part of the test lessons. The game is presented before the test. Fact games give students a great deal of practice with facts and rule applications. The games are important because many oral tasks presented during the regular lessons are answered by individuals, not by the whole group, which means that the students may not receive sufficient practice with many tasks.

Some facts are particularly troublesome for many students. The games provide intensive practice on these facts, but do so in a context that is reinforcing. The games become a combination of work and fun.

Groups of four players and a monitor play the game. (More than one group can play simultaneously.) Each group has a question sheet (or sheets) with 11 items numbered 2 through 12. The teacher reproduces these Fact Game sheets from blackline masters located in Appendix G.

To take a turn, a player rolls two dice (or number cubes). The player then adds the numbers on the cubes together, reads the item that corresponds to that number total (2 through 12), and responds to the item (which may involve answering several questions).

An assigned student monitor refers to the answer key in the back of the textbook and indicates whether the answer is correct. If so, the player earns a point and a checkmark is made on the student's scorecard. After 10 minutes, direct all students who earn more than 10 points to stand up.

On the next page is the fact game from lesson 30 and scorecard 30.

Reproducible Fact-Game scorecard sheets appear at the back of each workbook and at the back of this guide. Each student needs a copy for lessons 10 through 140.

Introducing the First Fact Game

The instructions for the first game (lesson 10) specify that you will be the monitor and demonstrate with four players how the game is played. When demonstrating the game, make sure that you model fast pacing, correct procedures, and appropriate responses to the players.

After demonstrating a few "rounds" of the game, assign students to permanent groups. Ideally, a group should consist of four players and a monitor. In some situations, you may have to form a group that consists of three or five players and a monitor. If possible, try to avoid larger groups. Each player in a larger group will receive fewer turns, and managing the group becomes more difficult.

Do not make groups homogeneous. (Do not place the better performers in one group and the lower performers in the other.) Rather, mix students of varying ability.

Assign monitors who are competent. The monitors should be good readers. Tell the monitors their responsibilities. They are to make sure that the players are taking turns, moving to the left. The monitor directs the player who is taking a turn to read the item aloud and answer it. Then the monitor confirms a correct response or gives the correct answer if the item was missed.

The next player does not roll the cubes until the preceding player has answered and has been told whether the response is correct. (If players are permitted to roll before the item is read and answered, they become so intent on getting ready for their turn that they do not listen to the preceding player's item and the answer.)

The fact game items appear on blackline masters (Appendix G near the back of this guide). Make one copy of the game for each group. Give each group two dice or number cubes.

Here are the procedures for playing:

- The monitor is the only person in a group who is permitted to look at the answer page at the back of the textbook.

- The other players take turns. A player rolls the cubes, adds the numbers showing, reads the item that has the same number, and tells the answer.

- If the player answers correctly, the monitor makes one tally mark on the player's scorecard. Or the monitor says, "Correct," and the player then makes one tally mark.

- The cubes go to the next player (the player to the left), and that player takes a turn.

Fact Game

2. Tell which footprint was made by:

   a. the lightest animal.

   b. the heaviest animal.

3. a. Whirlpools are made up of moving ▊.

   b. A whirlpool is shaped like a ▊.

4. Which came **later** on Earth:

   a. dinosaurs or strange sea animals?

   b. dinosaurs or horses?

Fact Game

5. Which layer went into the pile **later**:

   a. Layer C or layer A?

   b. Layer C or layer D?

6. Tell the letter of the layer that went into the pile:

   a. first

   b. next

   c. last

7. a. Tell the letter of the layer we live in.

   b. What's the name of layer **C?**

8. Tell the letter of the layer where we find:

   a. human skeletons

   b. horse skeletons

   c. dinosaur skeletons

9. As you touch each dinosaur, say the letter. Then tell the name of the dinosaur.

Fact Game

10. a. What kind of animals lived in the Mesozoic?

    b. Things closest to the bottom of the pile went into the pile ▊.

11. a. What are clouds made of?

    b. What kind of cloud does picture **C** show?

A   B   C

Lesson 30

1	2	3	4	5
6	7	8	9	10
11	12	13	14	15
16	17	18	19	20

Here are procedures for setting up the groups:

- If possible, provide a table for each group of players. There should be no obstructions that would prohibit the monitor from observing the players. Players should not be seated directly next to the monitor (where they could read the answers in the monitor's book).

- Each player's scorecard sheet should be on the table, ready for the game.

- If the monitor is to tally each player's correct answers, the monitor should have a pencil. If the monitor is to direct the players to make the tally marks, each player should have a pencil. **Note:** It is important that their scorecards are visible so the monitor can see whether the players are tallying correctly.

Observing the Fact Games

Follow these guidelines when you observe the games.

Reinforce a fast pace. Praise players who have the number cubes ready to roll, find the item quickly, read it correctly, and answer correctly. Remind the players that the faster they play, the more points they can earn. A fast pace also ensures that the players will be less likely to argue with the monitor.

Make comments about each group's progress: Look at how well you're doing. You've already played three rounds. Comments of this type are important because they let the students know that they are part of a group that is working together.

Do not permit the games to drag. If the groups are going slowly, do not tell the monitor, Come on, let's get this game moving. Nobody's going to earn very many points if they are this slow. A more positive, effective technique is to comment on games that are moving quickly: Wow, this group is really moving. Every player has had five turns already.

Make sure that players are following the rules. After the players have played the game for a few minutes, they may remember what item 5 is or what item 3 is. Therefore, they may attempt to answer the item without first reading the item aloud. For example, they'll say, "Number 10a. Dinosaurs," rather than reading the item, "What kind of animals lived in the Mesozoic?" Stop players who do not read the item aloud, and remind them of the rule: You must *read* the item aloud and *then* answer it. This stipulation is very important. Many items are included in the game because they are difficult for the students. The difficulty will be reduced greatly if a strong association between the item and the answer is established. This association is ensured, however, only if the students read the item aloud before answering it. Although the students may read it accurately to themselves, the other students in the group will not receive the benefit of hearing the item *and* the answer.

Make sure monitors award points only when the answers are correct. For nearly all items, the correct response is phrased in a very specific way, which is indicated in the answer key.

Unless the player's response is the same as that in the key, the response is incorrect. (There are a few items in later games that permit players to express an idea. For those items, the monitor must use some judgment. For most items, however, very little judgment is required.)

If an answer is not correct, the monitor is to read the correct answer aloud. Students are not permitted to argue with the monitor. If they argue, they lose a turn. The monitors are to raise their hand to signal a problem or a question they can't answer.

Stop the game after it has been played for 10 minutes. When only three minutes of playing time remain, tell the groups: Only 3 minutes more. When the time limit is up, tell the groups to stop: If a player has started a turn, finish that turn. Then the game is over.

Tell each group of players how well they did. Announce which groups played the game smoothly. Tell all students who have more than 10 points to stand up. Congratulate them.

In-Program Tests

Test lessons occur every ten lessons, beginning with lesson 10. Each test consists of content introduced and practiced in the preceding nine lessons. The tests also assess the vocabulary sentences that students have practiced.

In every test lesson students also play a fact game and do an individual reading checkout.

Test lessons that have both a written test and an individual reading checkout provide you with detailed performance information about individuals and about the group. The test shows you how well individuals and the group comprehend the content that was presented in the different selections, and also shows how well students perform on the skills and vocabulary being taught. The individual reading checkouts give information about how accurately and fluently students read. This package of information permits you to identify specific problems that individual students have, identify problems that are common to more than one student, and provide timely remedies.

Administering the Tests

1. Make sure that students have all materials they need: lined paper, textbook, and pencil.

2. Seat students so they cannot see the work of other students.

3. Direct students to complete the test and turn it in.

4. Score and grade the tests, and perform any necessary remedies before presenting the next lesson.

Scoring the Tests

There are different formats for marking the test, one of which is to perform a workcheck, during which students use a **marking pencil** to indicate which items are wrong (with an **X**). A variation is a workcheck in which students exchange tests and mark each others' tests. A third (and preferable) alternative is for you to score each test.

Even if you do not score each test, you should go over every test and make sure that the marking is accurate. After checking each student's test, write the total number of errors at the top of the test.

Recording Test Performance

You should record each student's performance in two places—on the Group Summary Chart (Appendix H) and on the Test Summary Sheet (Appendix I). A copy of the Test Summary Sheet for tests 1–7 appears below.

You record each student's performance by circling the number of each item the student missed. If the student missed items 3 and 18, you circle the numbers 3 and 18 for that student. The passing criterion for each test is shown at the bottom of the column for each test. Note that the criteria are not the same for different tests. (The criterion for test 2 is 26 correct out of 29, but the criterion for test 5 is 31 correct out of 34.) If the student fails the test, write **F** over the box with item numbers, or circle the box. Either system gives you a quick visual summary of the students who passed versus those who had trouble. In the Test 5 sample on page 69, Denise Barton has a failing score (29 correct out of 34 with passing criterion of 31/34) and so her error number has been circled.

TEST SUMMARY SHEET

Name	Test 1	Test 2	Test 3	Test 4	Test 5	Test 6	Test 7
	1 2 3 4 5 6 7 8 9 10 11 12 13 14 15 16 17 18 19 20 21 22 23 24 25 26 27 28 29 30 31 32 33 34 35	1 2 3 4 5 6 7 8 9 10 11 12 13 14 15 16 17 18 19 20 21 22 23 24 25 26 27 28 29	1 2 3 4 5 6 7 8 9 10 11 12 13 14 15 16 17 18 19 20 21 22 23 24 25 26 27 28 29 30 31 32 33 34 35 36	1 2 3 4 5 6 7 8 9 10 11 12 13 14 15 16 17 18	1 2 3 4 5 6 7 8 9 10 11 12 13 14 15 16 17 18 19 20 21 22 23 24 25 26 27 28 29 30 31 32 33 34	1 2 3 4 5 6 7 8 9 10 11 12 13 14 15 16 17 18 19 20 21 22 23 24 25 26 27 28 29 30 31 32 33 34 35 36	1 2 3 4 5 6 7 8 9 10 11 12 13 14 15 16 17 18 19 20 21 22 23 24 25 26 27 28 29 30 31 32 33 34 35 36
	1 2 3 4 5 6 7 8 9 10 11 12 13 14 15 16 17 18 19 20 21 22 23 24 25 26 27 28 29 30 31 32 33 34 35	1 2 3 4 5 6 7 8 9 10 11 12 13 14 15 16 17 18 19 20 21 22 23 24 25 26 27 28 29	1 2 3 4 5 6 7 8 9 10 11 12 13 14 15 16 17 18 19 20 21 22 23 24 25 26 27 28 29 30 31 32 33 34 35 36	1 2 3 4 5 6 7 8 9 10 11 12 13 14 15 16 17 18	1 2 3 4 5 6 7 8 9 10 11 12 13 14 15 16 17 18 19 20 21 22 23 24 25 26 27 28 29 30 31 32 33 34	1 2 3 4 5 6 7 8 9 10 11 12 13 14 15 16 17 18 19 20 21 22 23 24 25 26 27 28 29 30 31 32 33 34 35 36	1 2 3 4 5 6 7 8 9 10 11 12 13 14 15 16 17 18 19 20 21 22 23 24 25 26 27 28 29 30 31 32 33 34 35 36
	1 2 3 4 5 6 7 8 9 10 11 12 13 14 15 16 17 18 19 20 21 22 23 24 25 26 27 28 29 30 31 32 33 34 35	1 2 3 4 5 6 7 8 9 10 11 12 13 14 15 16 17 18 19 20 21 22 23 24 25 26 27 28 29	1 2 3 4 5 6 7 8 9 10 11 12 13 14 15 16 17 18 19 20 21 22 23 24 25 26 27 28 29 30 31 32 33 34 35 36	1 2 3 4 5 6 7 8 9 10 11 12 13 14 15 16 17 18	1 2 3 4 5 6 7 8 9 10 11 12 13 14 15 16 17 18 19 20 21 22 23 24 25 26 27 28 29 30 31 32 33 34	1 2 3 4 5 6 7 8 9 10 11 12 13 14 15 16 17 18 19 20 21 22 23 24 25 26 27 28 29 30 31 32 33 34 35 36	1 2 3 4 5 6 7 8 9 10 11 12 13 14 15 16 17 18 19 20 21 22 23 24 25 26 27 28 29 30 31 32 33 34 35 36
	1 2 3 4 5 6 7 8 9 10 11 12 13 14 15 16 17 18 19 20 21 22 23 24 25 26 27 28 29 30 31 32 33 34 35	1 2 3 4 5 6 7 8 9 10 11 12 13 14 15 16 17 18 19 20 21 22 23 24 25 26 27 28 29	1 2 3 4 5 6 7 8 9 10 11 12 13 14 15 16 17 18 19 20 21 22 23 24 25 26 27 28 29 30 31 32 33 34 35 36	1 2 3 4 5 6 7 8 9 10 11 12 13 14 15 16 17 18	1 2 3 4 5 6 7 8 9 10 11 12 13 14 15 16 17 18 19 20 21 22 23 24 25 26 27 28 29 30 31 32 33 34	1 2 3 4 5 6 7 8 9 10 11 12 13 14 15 16 17 18 19 20 21 22 23 24 25 26 27 28 29 30 31 32 33 34 35 36	1 2 3 4 5 6 7 8 9 10 11 12 13 14 15 16 17 18 19 20 21 22 23 24 25 26 27 28 29 30 31 32 33 34 35 36
	1 2 3 4 5 6 7 8 9 10 11 12 13 14 15 16 17 18 19 20 21 22 23 24 25 26 27 28 29 30 31 32 33 34 35	1 2 3 4 5 6 7 8 9 10 11 12 13 14 15 16 17 18 19 20 21 22 23 24 25 26 27 28 29	1 2 3 4 5 6 7 8 9 10 11 12 13 14 15 16 17 18 19 20 21 22 23 24 25 26 27 28 29 30 31 32 33 34 35 36	1 2 3 4 5 6 7 8 9 10 11 12 13 14 15 16 17 18	1 2 3 4 5 6 7 8 9 10 11 12 13 14 15 16 17 18 19 20 21 22 23 24 25 26 27 28 29 30 31 32 33 34	1 2 3 4 5 6 7 8 9 10 11 12 13 14 15 16 17 18 19 20 21 22 23 24 25 26 27 28 29 30 31 32 33 34 35 36	1 2 3 4 5 6 7 8 9 10 11 12 13 14 15 16 17 18 19 20 21 22 23 24 25 26 27 28 29 30 31 32 33 34 35 36
	1 2 3 4 5 6 7 8 9 10 11 12 13 14 15 16 17 18 19 20 21 22 23 24 25 26 27 28 29 30 31 32 33 34 35	1 2 3 4 5 6 7 8 9 10 11 12 13 14 15 16 17 18 19 20 21 22 23 24 25 26 27 28 29	1 2 3 4 5 6 7 8 9 10 11 12 13 14 15 16 17 18 19 20 21 22 23 24 25 26 27 28 29 30 31 32 33 34 35 36	1 2 3 4 5 6 7 8 9 10 11 12 13 14 15 16 17 18	1 2 3 4 5 6 7 8 9 10 11 12 13 14 15 16 17 18 19 20 21 22 23 24 25 26 27 28 29 30 31 32 33 34	1 2 3 4 5 6 7 8 9 10 11 12 13 14 15 16 17 18 19 20 21 22 23 24 25 26 27 28 29 30 31 32 33 34 35 36	1 2 3 4 5 6 7 8 9 10 11 12 13 14 15 16 17 18 19 20 21 22 23 24 25 26 27 28 29 30 31 32 33 34 35 36
	1 2 3 4 5 6 7 8 9 10 11 12 13 14 15 16 17 18 19 20 21 22 23 24 25 26 27 28 29 30 31 32 33 34 35	1 2 3 4 5 6 7 8 9 10 11 12 13 14 15 16 17 18 19 20 21 22 23 24 25 26 27 28 29	1 2 3 4 5 6 7 8 9 10 11 12 13 14 15 16 17 18 19 20 21 22 23 24 25 26 27 28 29 30 31 32 33 34 35 36	1 2 3 4 5 6 7 8 9 10 11 12 13 14 15 16 17 18	1 2 3 4 5 6 7 8 9 10 11 12 13 14 15 16 17 18 19 20 21 22 23 24 25 26 27 28 29 30 31 32 33 34	1 2 3 4 5 6 7 8 9 10 11 12 13 14 15 16 17 18 19 20 21 22 23 24 25 26 27 28 29 30 31 32 33 34 35 36	1 2 3 4 5 6 7 8 9 10 11 12 13 14 15 16 17 18 19 20 21 22 23 24 25 26 27 28 29 30 31 32 33 34 35 36
	1 2 3 4 5 6 7 8 9 10 11 12 13 14 15 16 17 18 19 20 21 22 23 24 25 26 27 28 29 30 31 32 33 34 35	1 2 3 4 5 6 7 8 9 10 11 12 13 14 15 16 17 18 19 20 21 22 23 24 25 26 27 28 29	1 2 3 4 5 6 7 8 9 10 11 12 13 14 15 16 17 18 19 20 21 22 23 24 25 26 27 28 29 30 31 32 33 34 35 36	1 2 3 4 5 6 7 8 9 10 11 12 13 14 15 16 17 18	1 2 3 4 5 6 7 8 9 10 11 12 13 14 15 16 17 18 19 20 21 22 23 24 25 26 27 28 29 30 31 32 33 34	1 2 3 4 5 6 7 8 9 10 11 12 13 14 15 16 17 18 19 20 21 22 23 24 25 26 27 28 29 30 31 32 33 34 35 36	1 2 3 4 5 6 7 8 9 10 11 12 13 14 15 16 17 18 19 20 21 22 23 24 25 26 27 28 29 30 31 32 33 34 35 36
Passing Criterion	32/35	26/29	32/36	16/18	31/34	32/36	32/36

GROUP SUMMARY CHART

Teacher **Ms. Turner**   Reading Mastery Plus Level 4   Group **2**

Lessons	41	42	43	44	CO 45	46	47	48	49	CO/Test 5	
Main Story Errors	11	12	10	12	(16)	11	10	14	12	████	
Name	IW	IW	IW	IW	CO	IW	IW	IW	IW	IW	CO	Test
Luis Cepeda	2	1	2	1	P / 0	2	1	0	1	3	P / 0	2
Yoko Higashi	(4)	3	2	2	P / 0	2	3	1	2	2	P / 1	2
Anita Diaz	1	1	1	0	P / 0	2	1	1	0	2	P / 0	0
Denise Barton	1	2	0	1	(F) / 1	1	0	1	0	2	P / 2	(5)
Zachary Gray	1	0	0	1	P / 0	1	2	1	1	1	P / 0	0
Eric Adler	2	1	1	0	P / 1	1	0	1	0	2	P / 1	2

You should also record each student's test performance on the Group Summary Chart. In the **Test** column, write the number of errors each student made on the test. Circle any number that exceeds the passing criterion for the test.

The sample Group Summary Chart above has been filled out for lessons 41 through 50 (test 5). The shaded column shows the part of the chart used for recording test 5 performance. (Denise Barton missed 5 out of 34 items. Her failing score has been circled.)

Test Remedies

Reproducible blackline masters of the Test Summary Sheets appear in Appendix I. The Test Summary Sheets provide an item-by-item analysis of the errors each student made. This information implies the kind of remedies that should be provided (ideally before you present the next lesson). A sample Test Summary for test 5 has been filled out and appears on the next page.

Total Errors

The total errors a student made tells you whether the student is progressing adequately. Students who exceed the specified number of errors are not performing at a level required to thoroughly comprehend the material they read.

Error Patterns

The basic patterns that you should look for when summarizing the data are: (a) a student (or groups of students) who fails the passing criterion on two or more consecutive tests; (b) the same item (or group of related items) being missed by more than 1/4 of the students.

Test Summary Sheet

Name	Test 5
Luis Cepeda	1 2 3 4 5 6 7 8 9 10 11 12 13 14 15 <u>16</u> 17 <u>18</u> 19 20 21 ㉒ 23 ㉔ 25 26 27 28 29 30 31 32 33 34
Yoko Higashi	1 2 3 4 5 6 7 8 9 10 11 12 13 14 15 16 17 <u>18</u> 19 20 21 22 23 ㉔ 25 26 ㉗ 28 29 30 31 32 33 34
Anita Diaz	1 2 3 4 5 6 7 8 9 10 11 12 13 14 15 16 17 18 19 20 21 22 23 24 25 26 27 28 29 30 31 32 33 34
Denise Barton	1 2 3 4 5 ⑥ 7 8 9 10 11 ⑫ 13 14 15 ⑯ 17 18 19 20 21 ㉒ 23 24 ㉕ 26 27 28 29 30 31 32 ㉝ 34
Zachary Gray	1 2 3 4 5 6 7 8 9 10 11 12 13 14 15 16 17 18 19 20 21 22 23 24 25 26 27 28 29 30 31 32 33 34
Eric Adler	1 2 3 4 5 6 7 8 9 10 11 12 13 <u>14</u> 15 <u>16</u> 17 <u>18</u> 19 ⑳ 21 ㉒ 23 24 25 <u>26</u> 27 28 29 30 31 32 33 34
	1 2 3 4 5 6 7 8 9 10 11 12 13 14 15 16 17 18 19 20 21 22 23 24 25 26 27 28 29 30 31 32 33 34
	1 2 3 4 5 6 7 8 9 10 11 12 13 14 15 16 17 18 19 20 21 22 23 24 25 26 27 28 29 30 31 32 33 34
Passing Criterion	**31/34**

Students Who Fail Consecutive Tests

Any student who fails consecutive tests is probably misplaced in the program. If more than one or two students exhibit this pattern, there are probably problems with the way the material is being presented, reviewed, and firmed. The first step in remediation would be to make

sure that the students are trying. The simplest way is to provide them with some sort of reward or positive response for meeting the criterion on tests. For example, make a chart that shows the number of students who pass each test. Have a party or some special award for students who pass two or more consecutive tests. Also make sure that you have a solid workcheck and that students are doing the fact games.

In some cases, you will have students who do not really belong in the program—based on their reading performance—and there is no possibility of putting them in another group. Although you teach carefully, these students still do not perform at criterion. The best practice in this case is to do what you can in firming these students and providing additional practice **outside the regular reading periods.** But when you are teaching the reading group, do not gear the rate of the presentation to these students. Rather, gear it to the students who are appropriately placed in the program. If you gear the presentation to the students who are misplaced, you will go far too slowly for the others, and the presentation will be boring.

Students Who Fail the Same Items

If 1/4 or more of the students fail the same item or group of related items, those items require more practice and review. Here are the remediation steps.

1. Identify the common items that are missed, and create a fact review that involves these items.

A Test Firming Table for each test appears in the teacher presentation book, at the end of the test lesson. You may use this table to help you construct fact reviews (or to firm specific concepts). The table lists the test items and indicates the first lesson in which that item appeared. Here is the table for test 5.

Test 5 Firming Table

Test Item	Introduced in lesson	Test Item	Introduced in lesson	Test Item	Introduced in lesson
1	43	13	45	25	47
2	43	14	45	26	47
3	43	15	45	27	47
4	44	16	45	28	39
5	44	17	45	29	43
6	44	18	45	30	43
7	44	19	45	31	46
8	44	20	45	32	39
9	44	21	45	33	43
10	45	22	46	34	39
11	45	23	46		
12	45	24	47		

According to the Test 5 summary sample on page 69, 1/4 of the students missed items 22 and 24.

22. What does an inventor get to protect an invention?

24. What are businesses that make things called?

By checking the Test 5 Firming Table, we see that item 22 was introduced in lesson 46, and item 24 in lesson 47.

Now create a fact review that involves these items. (See pages 56 and 57 and **Note** below.)

2. Present the fact review as part of the test remedy and then as part of subsequent lessons.

3. Present the items until the students are quite firm—virtually flawless.

4. If the number of students who had difficulties is large, present the review to the entire reading group.

Note: If students miss vocabulary items, you can follow a similar procedure in making up a fact review.

Sometimes, mistake patterns are predictable. If there has been a substitute for several lessons before the test, the students probably will perform more poorly than they would if you had been working with them. The remedy is not only to go over the information that relates to the items the students tended to miss, but also to go over information that is closely related. For example, if students tend to miss three items about the nervous system, they would probably miss other items about the nervous system that were not on the test. Go over the independent work for the lessons that introduce the nervous system, and identify all key items. (The Test Firming Table in the teacher presentation book indicates the key lessons where items are introduced.) Present those items in a fact-review format. (This review is probably best presented to the entire reading group, not to only those students who had serious problems.)

Use a variation of the same procedure if the pattern occurs on material that you had presented. Sometimes students get overloaded with information. First see if the items they miss are related. If they are, refer to the independent-work items, and identify all the major facts that are related to the items the students missed. Present those facts in a fact-review format.

After you have provided remedies, a general rule is to **retest students who failed.**

Do not retest the students after you simply mark answers on their test. Provide a remedy first. Before retesting make sure that they can respond correctly to the various items they missed. One purpose of the retest is to document that the remedy has worked. Another is to show the students that they can perform well on the tests and to provide them with the practice they need to achieve mastery.

Grades

The purpose of letter or number grades is to show the progress and skill level of the students. If students pass the tests consistently, and generally do not make more than three errors on their independent work, they deserve an A. The number grade would be over 90.

A student should be able to fail one or two tests and still earn an A. The reason is that some tests present difficult items.

The simplest grading system is to use the letter grades of A and F or U (for unsatisfactory). If students tend to meet criterion on independent work and tests, they receive an A. Otherwise, they receive a letter that suggests they are not performing adequately. Awarding Bs and Cs is difficult because the passing criteria for tests and independent work are quite high (sometimes above 90%). Students who average much below 90% are not performing adequately. If students do not meet the passing criteria for worksheets and tests, their percentage of correct responses may still be in the 80% range, but they are not performing at the level of mastery that is required by the program.

Language Arts Component

Directions and blackline masters for 140 lessons appear in the Language Arts Guide. These lessons occur daily.

The lessons in the Language Arts Guide are not to be presented during the reading period. Instead, up to 20 minutes per day should be scheduled at another point during the day.

Content

The language arts component is divided into 9 tracks. Each track has activities that occur on more than one lesson. Typically students will work on language arts activities from one track for two or more consecutive lessons. Then they'll work on activities from another track.

The language arts scope and sequence table shown on pages 72–74 shows the various tracks and lists the lessons for each track. Some of the tracks present a major emphasis. These tracks appear on many lessons. Other minor tracks appear on only a few lessons each.

Writing Narrative Accounts Based on Pictures

The track starts on lesson 7 and continues intermittently through lesson 93.

There are several different formats; however, all present a picture with directions about writing an account that is consistent with the picture. Students are to write stories that are interesting. They generally have to use "checks" to evaluate their work. For instance, here are the checks for the story on lesson 16:

- Did you tell what caused the boat to run into the rock?

Language Arts Skill	Lessons
Using commas	1–6, 10–13
Writing narrative accounts based on pictures	7, 9, 15, 16, 53, 55, 56, 91, 93
Writing on topics	8, 14, 17, 54, 92
Resource books	18–25, 31–33, 40–42, 113–116
Main idea/perspective	26–30, 34–39, 44–52, 57–67, 79–83, 101–109, 113–119, 121–140
Subject-verb agreement	40–43
Affixes and root words	68–78, 84–89, 95–100
Writing based on retelling	90, 94
Outlining	110–112
Rhetorical devices	117–124

- Did you tell what happened after the boat crashed into the rock?

- Did you tell what plan Clara and Kobe made to get help?

- Did you tell how their plan worked?

Writing on Topics

The track starts on lesson 8 and continues intermittently through lesson 92.

Each lesson presents a topic such as **My favorite holiday time of year.** In a short essay form, students identify their favorite holiday, explain why it is their favorite, and relate special experiences that they had during this holiday.

Resource Books

The track starts on lesson 18 and continues intermittently through lesson 116.

During the first lessons, students review information that they learned in level 3 about a dictionary. Students review the purpose of the dictionary, the different kinds of information the dictionary provides—how the word is pronounced, how many syllables it has, what the various meanings are and the parts of speech for the various meanings.

On later lessons students learn about two other reference books—the atlas and the encyclopedia. After learning the kind of information that each of these resource books offers, students use various resource books to find answers to questions like **What is the largest pyramid in Egypt?** and **What is the capital of France?** Later students write answers to questions that ask which type of resource book would be used to find specific information, such as the number of square miles in Texas, which Great Lakes touch Michigan, what the word **marginal** means.

Starting on lesson 113, students use a context clue to look up words in the dictionary and identify the meaning. For instance, they are told that one meaning of the word **crop** has to do with plants. Students look up the word **crop,** find the appropriate meaning, and copy it. Students then write the meaning of **crop** that has to do with cutting.

Main Idea/Perspectives

This is the dominant track in the language arts component. The track starts on lesson 26 and continues intermittently through lesson 140. It contains 72 lessons.

The track presents two types of activities:

1. The students copy a main-idea sentence such as, Leonard talked to people about inventions they wanted. Students write more sentences that provide supporting details for this main idea.

2. Students pretend that they are another person and write specific accounts from that person's perspective. For instance, Pretend that you are Grandmother Esther, and you are wearing your exercise outfit. Write at least three sentences that tell why you are wearing that outfit. You could tell where you plan to exercise and what exercises you will do.

Affixes and Root Words

The track starts on lesson 68 and continues intermittently through lesson 100.

Students first review the affixes they learned in level 3: **dis, re, un, less, ful, ness, er, super.** They then learn three new affixes: **able, mis, ly.** For the affix, they learn a meaning. For instance, the meaning taught for **ly** is **in that way.** So the word that means **in a quick way** is **quickly.**

Students learn the categories **prefix, root,** and **suffix.** Near the end of the track, they analyze words by marking the prefix, the root, and the suffix, for instance un (happi) ness.

Rhetorical Devices

This track provides instruction on similes, metaphors, and alliteration. The track begins on lesson 117 and goes through lesson 124. For similes (Her teeth were like pearls), students identify the two things that are the same in a simile and how those two things are the same.

Metaphors are taught as devices that are like similes but that do not use the words **like** or **as** (Her teeth were pearls). The exercises require students to identify what two things are the same and how they are the same. Students also identify whether sentences are similes or metaphors.

For alliteration students are presented with a word and then identify words that alliterate with that word. For instance, words that alliterate with the word **sheep— shoe, ship, she, shop.**

Commas

The track starts on lesson 1 and ends on lesson 13. Students learn the rules for using commas when writing words in a series (connected by **and** or **or**), dates, and addresses.

Subject-Verb Agreement

The track starts on lesson 40 and continues through lesson 43. Students complete sentences using the correct verb, for instance, This thin man _____ every day. (swim   swims)

Writing Based on Retelling

This track occurs on two lessons, lesson 90 and lesson 94. The exercises require students to retell the first part of a story and then make up an ending. You read the first part to them two times. Then they write the whole story. They don't have to use the same sentences that you present; however, their retelling of the first part should contain all the important details that you present. This activity is parallel to the picture activities, except that the background information is provided through words, not a picture.

Outlining

The track starts on lesson 110 and continues through lesson 112. Students identify the main ideas of a topic and then construct an outline that has each main idea listed with supporting details under it. For instance students make an outline for the title "When I Was Younger." Students identify three different ages that they will use. These are the main heads of the outline. Under each main head, they write some details about things they did and liked at that age.

Literature Component

Literature Lessons

The literature component of *Reading Mastery Plus* Level 4 consists of a presentation book, *Literature Guide*, two "Read-to" books, and copies of the student literature anthology that are used in the 15 literature lessons. The presentation book includes directions for the lessons and blackline masters that are to be reproduced as student material.

Literature activities are scheduled as part of every tenth lesson, starting with Lesson 10. In addition, there are two supplementary novels with questions and blackline masters. These two books may be presented after students have completed lesson 140 in *Reading Mastery Plus* Level 4.

All but two of the literature lessons are scheduled every 10 lessons, starting with lesson 10, and follow each 10-lesson test with an additional selection after lesson 135. The literature lesson does not have to be scheduled on the same day as the test, and it should not be scheduled as part of the regular reading lesson. The literature lessons are a treat. Schedule each activity for 40–80 minutes. The lessons with a "Read-to" selection (lessons 50, 60, and 120) may be presented on two separate days.

Literature Selections

Literature lessons present stories, poems, and a play. The following chart lists the selections and the lessons in which they are to be presented.

Materials

In addition to the anthologies and the blackline masters, students need specific materials for the scheduled activities. The teacher presentation for each lesson in the Literature Guide specifies what materials are needed. (The major supplies that students need for these lessons are lined paper, crayons, scissors, tape, and paste.)

Presented with Lesson	Title	Author
10	The Velveteen Rabbit	Harriet Winfield
20	Dreams	Langston Hughes
	The Runner	Faustin Charles
30	The Emperor's New Clothes	Harvey Cleaver
40	Why Leopard Has Black Spots	Told by Won-Ldy Paye
50	Boar Out There	Cynthia Rylant
	Crossing the Creek	Laura Ingalls Wilder
60	Camp on the High Prairie	Laura Ingalls Wilder
	Spaghetti	Cynthia Rylant
70	Charlie Best	Ruth Corrin
80	The Pancake Collector	Jack Prelutsky
90	Not Just Any Ring	Danita Ross Haller
100	A Lucky Thing	Alice Schertle
	The New Kid	Mike Makley
110	Steps	Deborah M. Newton Chocolate
120	The Soup Stone	Retold by Maria Leach
	Julie Rescues Big Mack	Roger Hall
130	Amelia Bedelia	Peggy Parish
135	My (Wow!) Summer Vacation	Susan Cornell Poskanzer
140	The Story of Daedalus and Icarus	Fran Lehr
Supplementary Novels	The Chalk Box Kid Pirate Island Adventure	Clyde Robert Bulla Peggy Parish

Preparation

Before presenting each literature lesson, read the scheduled activity, secure the materials, and copy the blackline masters.

Presenting the Lessons

Each literature lesson is based on a theme from the selection. The following chart lists the lesson themes and gives a brief summary of the primary expansion activities for each lesson.

Literature Lesson	Presented with Lesson	Theme	Primary Expansion Activities
1. *The Velveteen Rabbit*	10	Love	Students write about their favorite "soft and cuddly."
2-1. *Dreams*	20	Dream metaphors	Students make up additional parts of the poem; students draw pictures of dreams.
2-2. *The Runner*	20	Fantastic ability	Students draw a picture about running fast.
3. *The Emperor's New Clothes*	30	Admitting the truth	Students write a sequel to the story.
4. *Why Leopard Has Black Spots*	40	Deceit	Students write and illustrate a story about how another animal got its stripes; students create pictures that demonstrate animal camouflage.
5-1. *Boar Out There*	50	Fear	Students produce a map of the story; students discuss the story characters' fears; students write about their own fear.
5-2. (Read to) *Crossing the Creek**	50*	Fear	None
6-1. (Read to) *Camp on the High Prairie**	60*	Being safe	None
6-2. *Spaghetti*	60	What makes life worthwhile	Students discuss the changes in how the main character feels through the story; students write about the kind of place they'd like to live in.
7. *Charlie Best*	70	What's the evidence?	Students write a new "chapter" for the story, following established patterns of the story characters.
8. *The Pancake Collector*	80	Collections	Students write about a collection they would like to have.
9. *Not Just Any Ring*	90	Courage	Students research Native Americans of the southwest; students make clay models of different story locations.

10-1. *A Lucky Thing*	100	Perspective	Students write about things that might make somebody look lucky to somebody else.
10-2. *The New Kid*	100	Gender equality	None
11. *Steps*	110	Overcoming differences	Students write a play about characters who disagree about something; students discuss the relative importance of little problems when a big problem occurs.
12-1. *The Soup Stone*	120	Combined efforts; big changes can happen in small steps.	Students develop a recipe that involves an ingredient that doesn't change what the recipe produces; students discuss the group effort demonstrated in the story; students write an ending to a story that involves a group effort.
12-2. (Read to) *Julie Rescues Big Mack**	120*	Clues; mistreating animals	Students discuss potential behavior outcomes for the animal character and how the human characters can help the animal; students discuss story clues.
13. *Amelia Bedelia*	130	Unclear instructions	Students draw pictures for different interpretations of a set of unclear instructions.
14. *My (Wow!) Summer Vacation*	135	Achieving personal goals	Students write about their favorite vacation; students produce a map for the story.
15. *The Story of Daedalus and Icarus*	140	Disobedience	Students make or gather props, stage settings and costumes, and then put on a reading version of the play.

APPENDIX A–PLACEMENT

Administering the Placement Test

As a rule, students who have performed well in a third grade reading program should be able to succeed in *Reading Mastery Plus* Level 4. However, this rule may not apply to all students, particularly those who can decode words silently but cannot read aloud with sufficient accuracy (no more than two errors per 100 words). Also, students who are extremely weak in answering written comprehension questions should not go into *Reading Mastery Plus* Level 4.

The placement test on page 82 determines the rate-accuracy and comprehension performance of students. Administer the test to all the students before placing them in the program. The test results will provide you with:

- "baseline" information about their reading rate and accuracy

- a basis for evaluating their improvement after they have completed the program

- a means of identifying students who may be placed in the program "on trial," and those who should not be placed in the program.

Part 1 of the test is to be administered individually to the students. They should not observe others taking the test. Part 1 requires about two minutes per student. You will need a stop watch. *If students make more than six errors on Part 1, do not administer Part 2 to those students.*

Part 2 of the test may be presented to more than one student at the same time. Part 2 requires the students to write answers to comprehension questions about the Part 1 passage.

Instructions for Part 1

Reproduce the one-page Placement Test that appears on page 82. Make one copy for each student that you are to test.

1. Call a student to a corner of the room, where the test will be given.

2. Give a copy of the test to the student.

3. Point to the column of words at the top of the test. Tell the student: "Touch word 1." (Wait.) "That word is California."

4. Repeat step 3 for words 2–5.

5. Point to the passage in part 1.

6. Tell the student: "You're going to read this passage out loud. I want you to read it as well as you can. Don't try to read it so fast that you make mistakes. But don't read it so slowly that it doesn't make any sense. You have two minutes to read the passage. Go."

7. Time the student. If the student takes more than three seconds on a word, say the word, count it as an error, and permit the student to continue reading. To record errors, make one tally mark for each error.

Count all the following behaviors as errors:

- Misreading a word (Count as one error.)

- Omitting a word part (Listen carefully for *s* and *ed*.) (Count as one error.)

- Sounding out a word but not saying the word at a normal speaking rate (Count as one error.)

- Skipping a word (Count as one error.)

- Skipping a line (Immediately show the student the correct line.) (Count as one error.)

- Not identifying a word within three seconds (Tell the word.) (Count as one error.)

- Reading a word incorrectly and then reading it correctly (Count as one error.)

Also count each word not read by the end of the two-minute time limit as an error. For example, if the student is eight words from the end of the passage by the end of the time limit, count eight errors.

Instructions for Part 2

After you've administered Part 1 to all the students, present Part 2 to those students who made no more than six errors on Part 1. (Part 2 is a group test.)

1. Assemble the students.

2. Give each student a copy of the placement test.

3. Make sure the students have pencils.

4. Give the group these instructions: "These are questions about the passage that you read earlier. Write the answers to the comprehension items at the bottom of your paper. You have five minutes to finish the questions."

5. Collect the test sheets after five minutes.

Answer Key Part 2

1. *Idea:* Because the ship was on fire
2. Linda, Kathy   3. lifeboats
4. Linda   5. 13   6. 10   7. hand
8. Idea: In a lifeboat   9. Japan
10. Idea: To see their father   11. 3 days

Placement Criteria

Use the table below to determine placement for each student.

Errors	Placement
If a student makes seven errors or more on Part 1 **OR** three errors or more on Part 2	Place the student in a reading-language program more elementary than *Reading Mastery Plus* Level 4
If a student makes no more than six errors on Part 1 **AND** no more than two errors on Part 2	Place the student at *Reading Mastery Plus* Level 4, lesson 1

If you suspect that some students are too advanced for the program (students who score 0 or 1 on the placement test and who exhibit good comprehension skills), present the main story from lesson 103 to them. Present the tasks specified for the main story oral reading, and assign items 1–10 (17 responses) from lesson 103 in the workbook.

If the student makes no more than eight story-reading errors and no more than two workbook errors on lesson 103, place the student in a higher-level program, *Reading Mastery Plus* Level 5.

Remedies

- If students fail Part 1, they are weak in decoding. The simplest remedy for these students is to select material that they are able to read without making more than two errors per 100 words. Set rate criterion for these students (based on the rate at which they are able to read making no more than two errors per 100 words) and as they improve, change the criterion so they are required to read faster. Continue to provide lots of practice until the students read at the minimum rate of 100 words per minute without making more than two errors per 100 words.

- If students fail Part 2, provide practice on basic comprehension questions (who, what, when, where, why). Direct these students to read aloud. Ask questions after each sentence. Make sure that each question can be clearly answered by the passage that the students read. Provide this kind of practice until the students are proficient at answering questions.

When you feel the students are firm on skills that were initially deficient, readminister the placement test.

Name _____

READING MASTERY PLUS LEVEL 4 PLACEMENT TEST

Part 1

"Fire! Fire!" a voice said over the loudspeaker. "The forward deck is on fire," the voice announced. "Everybody, leave the ship. Get into the lifeboats!"

Linda and her sister were on their way from the United States to Japan. Linda was thirteen years old, three years older than Kathy. Their father was in Japan, and they were on their way to visit him. Three days before, they had left California on a great ship called an ocean liner. They were now somewhere in the middle of the Pacific Ocean.

"Fire! Fire!" the voice shouted. "Everybody get into the lifeboats!"

People were running this way and that way on the deck of the ship. They were yelling and crying.

"Hold on to my hand," Linda said. The girls went to the lifeboats. People were all around them, shoving and yelling. Linda could not see much. She was afraid. Suddenly she was no longer holding Kathy's hand.

Suddenly a strong pair of arms grabbed Linda. "In you go," a voice said. A big man picked Linda up and put her in the lifeboat.

"Where's my sister?" Linda asked. Linda looked but she couldn't see her younger sister.

1. California
2. Pacific
3. lifeboat
4. Japan
5. loudspeaker

1. Why was everybody trying to leave the ship? _____

2. Name the two sisters that were on the ship. _____

3. People were trying to get into the _____

4. Which sister was older? _____

5. How old was that girl? _____

6. How old was her sister? _____

7. Linda told Kathy, "Hold on to my _____."

8. When the big man picked up Linda, where did he put her? _____

9. What country were the girls going to? _____

10. Why were the girls going there? _____

11. How long had they been on the ship? _____

Part 2

82   *Appendix A—Placement*

APPENDIX B–SPECIAL PROJECTS

PROJECT	AFTER LESSON	MATERIALS
Geese flight path from Canada to Florida	10	Unlined paper and pencils
Map distance work; prediction story	12	Road maps (with mileage key) of students' state
Eskimo wall chart	22	Reference materials (books on Alaska, books on Eskimos, encyclopedias, *National Geographic* magazines, CD-ROMs); note cards; drawing paper and poster-making supplies (butcher paper or poster board, markers, crayons, paints, scissors, paste)
Dinosaur wall chart	35	Reference materials (books on dinosaurs, books on the Mesozoic era, encyclopedias, CD-ROMs) and poster-making supplies (butcher paper or poster board, markers, crayons, paints, scissors, paste, magazines for pictures)
Leonard's new invention	52	Crayons, colored pencils, lined paper, and Workbook A page 94
Solar system wall chart (sun and first 5 planets)	66	Reference materials (books on the solar system, encyclopedias, CD-ROMs) and poster-making supplies (butcher paper or poster board, markers, crayons, paints, scissors, paste, magazines for pictures)
Train an animal to do a new trick	84	Books on animal training
Iditarod scavenger hunt	100	Iditarod Web site (www.Iditarod.com), magazines, newspapers, books on Iditarod
Solar system wall chart (remaining 4 planets)	106	Reference materials (books on the solar system, encyclopedias, CD-ROMs) and poster-making supplies (butcher paper or poster board, markers, crayons, paints, scissors, paste, magazines for pictures)
Molecule wall chart, molecule models	111	Reference materials (books on matter and molecules, encyclopedias, CD-ROMs) Optional materials: Poster-making supplies (butcher paper or poster board, markers, crayons, paints, scissors, paste, magazines for pictures); model-making supplies (styrofoam balls, toothpicks, paints)
Find pictures of deep-sea fish	116	Reference materials (books on ocean life, encyclopedias, CD-ROMs) Optional materials: Poster-making supplies (butcher paper or poster board, markers, crayons, paints, scissors, paste, magazines for pictures)
Presentations of the human body, the poles, the Milky Way	140	Library books, pencils, and lined paper

APPENDIX C—MODEL VOCABULARY SENTENCES

LESSON INTRODUCED	SENTENCE NUMBER	SENTENCE
3	1	The horses became restless on the dangerous route.
12	2	Scientists do not ignore ordinary things.
16	3	She actually repeated that careless mistake.
21	4	The smell attracted flies immediately.
25	5	The rim of the volcano exploded.
29	6	The new exhibit displayed mysterious fish.
33	7	She automatically arranged the flowers.
36	8	They were impressed by her large vocabulary.
39	9	He responded to her clever solution.
43	10	The patent attorney wrote an agreement.
46	11	The applause interrupted his speech.
49	12	She selected a comfortable seat.
53	13	Without gravity, they were weightless.
56	14	She demonstrated how animals use oxygen.
59	15	Lava erupted from the volcano's crater.
64	16	The incredible whales made them anxious.
67	17	The boring speaker disturbed the audience.
71	18	A lot of folks mobbed the cute singer.
74	19	The tour to the islands was a fantastic experience.
78	20	She will contact the person we want to hire.
83	21	I have confidence that we can avoid a long conversation.
86	22	The scuba diver and her partner surfaced near the reef.
91	23	The veterinarian gave the dogs a thorough examination.
95	24	Visibility was miserable in the fierce blizzard.
102	25	At midnight, he saw a familiar galaxy.
106	26	The crystal contained more than a billion molecules.
111	27	The poem they created was nonsense.
114	28	The squid wriggled its tentacles.
117	29	The triceps muscle is bigger than the biceps muscle.
122	30	The injury to his spinal cord paralyzed him.
127	31	A single star was near the horizon.
132	32	Troops of baboons moved across the veld.

APPENDIX D–STUDENT GLOSSARY

actually   *Actually* means *really.*

adventure   An *adventure* is a new, exciting experience.

Africa   *Africa* is a large area of land that is bigger than North America.

agreement   An *agreement* is a paper that tells what two people promise to do.

Andros Island   *Andros Island* is an island that is close to Florida.

anxious   *Anxious* is another word for *nervous* or *scared.*

appear   Something *appears* when it first comes into sight.

applause   *Applause* is another word for the *clapping.*

approach   When you *approach* something, you move toward it.

arithmetic   *Arithmetic* is another word for *math.*

armor   *Armor* is a hard covering that is made to protect anything inside the armor.

arrange   When you *arrange* things, you put them where you want them.

assigned   A person who is *assigned* a book is the only person who can use the book.

assignment   A job that somebody gives you to do is called an *assignment.*

Atlantic Ocean   The *Atlantic Ocean* is the ocean that touches the eastern shore of the United States.

attorney   An *attorney* is a *lawyer.*

attracted   If you are *attracted* to something, you are really interested in that thing.

audience   All the people who watch an event are the people in the *audience.*

automatically   Things that happen *automatically* don't require any thought.

Bermuda Triangle   The *Bermuda Triangle* is an area in the Atlantic Ocean where very strange things have happened to ships.

blisters *Blisters* are sore bubbles that form from rubbing or burning.

boring *Boring* is the opposite of *interesting.*

bow The *bow* of the ship is the front of a ship.

breath Your *breath* is the air you take in or let out.

business If you sell flowers, you are in the *business* of selling flowers.

careless *Careless* is the opposite of *careful.*

character When you say that somebody is a *character,* you mean the person is unusual.

checker A person or a machine that checks things is called a *checker.*

chuckle A *chuckle* is a little laugh.

clearing A *clearing* is a place in a forest or a jungle where there are no trees.

clever *Clever* is another word for very smart.

cliff A *cliff* is like a side of a hill that goes almost straight up and down.

comfortable Things that are *comfortable* feel very pleasant.

conclude *Conclude* is another word for *finish.*

constant Something that is *constant* doesn't change.

crater A volcano's *crater* is the enormous dent in the top of the volcano.

crooked *Crooked* is the opposite of *straight.*

current A water *current* is a stream of water that moves in the same direction.

danger Something that's a *danger* is something that is not safe.

dart When something *darts* around, it moves like a dart, very fast and straight.

daydream When you *daydream,* you think about things that you would like to be doing.

deliver When you bring something to a place, you *deliver* it to that place.

demonstrate When you *demonstrate* something, you show it.

device A *device* is a machine or fixture that is made by people.

diagram A *diagram* is a picture that is something like a map.

direct When you *direct* people to do something, you order them to do it.

disappointed   When something you want does not happen, you feel *disappointed.*

display   Another word for *show* is *display.*

disturb   When you bother something, you *disturb* it.

divided   Things that are *divided* are separated into parts.

dome   Another word for a *rounded ceiling* is a *dome.*

electricity   *Electricity* is the power that runs appliances like washing machines and televisions.

embarrassed   When you are *embarassed,* you feel foolish or silly.

energy   The amount of work something can do depends on how much *energy* it has.

engineer   The *engineer* on a ship is the crew member who makes sure that the engine is running well.

equator   The *equator* is a make-believe line around the middle of the earth.

equipment   The supplies or tools needed to do something is the *equipment* needed to do it.

equipped   When you're well *equipped* for doing something, you have all the supplies you need to do the job.

erupted   When lava *erupts* from a volcano, the lava is spit or coughed out.

Eskimo   *Eskimos* are native people that live in Alaska and Canada.

example   A dog is an *example* of an animal.

excellent   Something that is very, very good is *excellent.*

exhibit   An *exhibit* has things arranged for people to see.

expect   When you *think* something will happen, you *expect* it to happen.

explanation   When you give an *explanation,* you tell how something works.

explode   When things *explode,* they make a loud bang and fly apart.

expression   The *expression* on your face shows what you're feeling.

faint   If something is *faint,* it is very hard to hear or see.

female   Girls and women are called *females.*

first mate   The *first mate* is a crew member who is the captain's main helper.

flock   A *flock* of birds is a group of birds that lives together and flies together.

Florida   *Florida* is one of the states in the United States.

foolish   Something that is *foolish* is the opposite of *wise.*

funnel-shaped   Things that are *funnel-shaped* are shaped like a round tube that is wide on one end and narrow on the other end.

galley   The *galley* is the kitchen on an airplane or ship.

gallon   A *gallon* is a unit of measurement that is the same as four quarts.

gases   *Gases* float in the air.

gather   When you pick up things from different places and put hem in one place, you *gather* those things.

gentle   Things that are *gentle* are the opposite of things that are rough.

glance   When you *glance* at something, you give that thing a quick look.

glide   When a bird *glides,* it goes through the air without flapping or moving its wings.

gravity   *Gravity* is the force that pulls things back to Earth.

grinding   When two hard things rub together, they *grind,* and they make a *grinding* sound.

guest   A *guest* is a visitor.

gulp   When you *gulp* something, you swallow it quickly.

hardened   Something that becomes hard is called *hardened.*

hesitate   When you *hesitate,* you pause for a moment.

hind   Another word for the *back* part of animals is the *hind* part.

hitch   When you *hitch* two things together, you attach them to each other.

however   Another word for *but* is *however.*

ice floe   An *ice floe* is a flat sheet of ice that floats in the ocean.

ignore   When you don't pay attention to something, you *ignore* that thing.

immediately   *Immediately* means *right now.*

impressed   When you're *impressed* by something, you think it is very good.

incredible *Incredible* is another word for *amazing.*

interest If you have an *interest* in something, you pay attention to that thing.

interrupt *Interrupt* means *break into.*

invent When a person makes an object for very first time, the person *invents* the object.

invisible If something is *invisible,* you can't see it.

Io *Io* is a large moon that circles Jupiter.

Jupiter *Jupiter* is one of the planets in the solar system.

kayak A *kayak* is a small boat with an opening in the center for a person.

Kentucky *Kentucky* is a state that you might go through if you went from Michigan to Florida.

kneel When you *kneel,* you get down on your knees.

lava *Lava* is hot melted rock.

lawyer People who need help with the law go to a *lawyer.*

leathery If something is *leathery,* it looks or feels like leather.

male Men and boys are called *males.*

manage If you *manage* to do something, you work hard until you do it.

manufacturer Somebody who makes a product is a *manufacturer* of the product.

mast A *mast* on a ship is a tall pole.

mention When you *mention* something, you quickly tell about it.

Michigan *Michigan* is one of the states that touches Canada.

migration A *migration* is a long journey that animals make every year.

moan A *moan* is a sound that people make when they are in pain.

mukluks *Mukluks* are very warm boots that Eskimos wear.

museum A *museum* is a place with many different kinds of exhibits.

mysterious Things that you do not understand are *mysterious.*

no-see-ums *No-see-ums* are tiny biting insects that live in Alaska and Canada.

nudge   When you *nudge* something, you give it a little push.

numb   When part of your body gets *numb,* you don't have any feeling in that part.

ordinary   Things that you see all the time in different places are *ordinary* things.

owe   Something that you *owe* is something that you must pay.

oxygen   *Oxygen* is the part of the air your body needs to survive.

pace   The *pace* of something is the speed of that thing.

pale   If something is *pale*, it is whiter than it normally is.

palms   The insides of your hands are called *palms.*

patent   A *patent* is a license that says that only one person can make a particular product.

patent attorney   A *patent attorney* is a lawyer whose special job is getting patents for new inventions.

pebbled   Things that are *pebbled* are covered with small stones.

permission   Someone who has approval to do something has *permission* to do it.

planet   The earth that we live on is a *planet.*

possible   Things that are *possible* are things that could happen.

practice   When you *practice* something, you work on it.

prepare   When you get ready for something, you *prepare* for that thing.

pressure   *Pressure* is a push.

products   Things that are made by people are *products.*

protection   *Protection* is something that protects.

purchase   *Purchase* is another word for *buy.*

quake   When something *quakes,* it shakes very hard.

receive   *Receive* means *get.*

remains   The *remains* of something are the parts that are left.

repeat   When you *repeat* something, you do it again and again and again.

respond   *Respond* is another word for *react.*

restless   When you feel *restless* you don't want to keep doing what you're doing.

ridge   A *ridge* is a long strip of land that is raised above the land around it.

ridiculous   When you think something is really silly, you think it is *ridiculous.*

rim   Things with a thin top edge have a *rim.*

rose   Something that moved up yesterday *rose* yesterday.

route   The different ways you can go to get to a place are the different *routes* that you can take to get there.

scientists   *Scientists* are highly-trained people who study different things about the world.

scrambled   Things that are *scrambled* are all mixed up.

seagulls   *Seagulls* are birds that are seen around the ocean.

section   *Section* is another word for part.

select   When you *select* something, you choose it.

sense   If you have a good *sense* of sight, you can see well.

serious   The opposite of something funny is something *serious.*

shaft   The *shaft* of a pencil is the part with long straight sides.

shallow   *Shallow* is the opposite of *deep.*

sharp-minded   A person who is *sharp-minded* has a quick mind or a smart mind.

shrank   Things that get smaller now shrink; things that got smaller yesterday *shrank.*

shriek   A *shriek* is a very sharp scream.

sight   A *sight* is something you see.

sir   An important man is sometimes called *sir.*

slosh   If you swing a bucket of water back and forth, the water *sloshes* around.

slump   When people *slump,* they slouch and do not sit up straight or stand up straight.

solar system   The *solar system* is the group of planets and moons that move around the sun.

solution   The *solution* to a problem is how to solve the problem.

solve   When you *solve* a problem, you figure out the answer to that problem.

son   If parents have a male child, that child is the parents' *son.*

speckled   Things that have small spots are *speckled.*

splatter   When wet things hit something, they *splatter* and spread out.

sprang   If an animal jumped at something yesterday, it *sprang* yesterday.

stern   The *stern* of a ship is the back of the ship.

stern   A *stern* expression is a frowning expression.

stumble   When you *stumble,* you trip.

suggest   When you *suggest* a plan, you tell about a possible plan.

supplies   The *supplies* you need for a job are the things you'll use up when you do that job.

suppose   Another word for *believe* or *think* is *suppose.*

surface   The *surface* of the water is the top of the water.

surround   If something *surrounds* you, it is all the way around you.

survive   If you *survive,* you *live.*

swarm   When insects *swarm,* hundreds of them fly very close to each other.

swift   Something that is *swift* is very fast.

tangle   A *tangle* is a mixed-up mass.

telescope   A *telescope* is a device that makes distant things look large.

throat   The front of your neck is sometimes called your *throat.*

Tokyo   *Tokyo* is the largest city in Japan.

tone   Your *tone* of voice tells what you are feeling.

tremble   Something that *trembles* shakes a little.

trout   A *trout* is a fish.

tumble   When things *tumble,* they turn over and over and over.

unfasten   When you *unfasten* something, you undo it.

Uranus   *Uranus* is one of the planets in the solar system.

vocabulary   A person's *vocabulary* is all the words the person knows.

volcano A *volcano* is a mountain that is made from hot flowing rock that comes from inside the earth.

weightless Things that are *weightless* float in space.

whales *Whales* are warm-blooded animals that live in the ocean.

whether In some sentences, *whether* means *if*.

wrist Your *wrist* is the joint between your hand and your arm.

absolutely   *Absolutely* is another word for *totally* or *completely.*

according   If you do something that follows the rules, you do that thing *according* to the rules.

addressed   When letters are *addressed* to you, they have your name and address on them.

admission   The amount you pay to get into a show is the *admission* for that show.

aimlessly   When you do things *aimlessly,* you don't have a plan about what you're doing.

amuse   When something *amuses* a person, it makes the person laugh.

anchor   An *anchor* is a weight that is attached to a boat.

Anchorage   *Anchorage* is the name of a city in Alaska.

arrangements   When you make *arrangements* to do something, you make a plan to do that thing.

assistant   An *assistant* is somebody who helps the person who is in charge.

attractive   *Attractive* is another word for *pretty.*

avoid   When you *avoid* something, you stay away from that thing.

award   An *award* is something you receive for doing something special.

baboon   *Baboons* are a kind of monkey.

backbone   The bones that run from your skull down the middle of your back are called the *backbone.*

balanced   When things are *balanced* on a point, they don't tip one way or the other way.

bare   When something is *bare,* it has no coverings.

barracuda   A *barracuda* is a large arrow-shaped fish with sharp teeth.

beak   The bill of a bird is called a *beak.*

beware   *Beware* is another word for *watch out.*

biceps   The *biceps* is the muscle on the front of the upper arm.

billion   A *billion* is a thousand millions.

blizzard A *blizzard* is a snowstorm that is windy and very cold.

blood vessel A *blood vessel* is a tube that carries blood through the body.

briskly *Briskly* means *fast and peppy.*

buoyancy device A *buoyancy device* is something a diver wears to control how buoyant the diver is underwater.

buoyant Things that are *buoyant* float.

cell *Cells* are the smallest parts of your body.

cerebrum The part of the brain that lets you think is called the *cerebrum.*

certificate A *certificate* is a paper that proves something.

challenging Another word for *very difficult* is *challenging.*

chamber Special rooms are called *chambers.*

chant When you *chant,* you say the same thing over and over.

chilly *Chilly* means *sort of cold.*

comment When you *comment* about something, you tell about that thing.

compass A *compass* is a tool that shows the directions north, south, east and west.

compete Things that *compete* with each other are in a contest with each other.

confidence When you have *confidence* about something, you are *sure* about it.

congratulate When you *congratulate* somebody, you praise the person for something the person did well.

conversation When people talk to each other about something, they have a *conversation* about that thing.

coral The shells of animals that cover rocks in the ocean are called *coral.*

courage Another word for *bravery* is *courage.*

create *Create* is another word for *make.*

cruel *Cruel* is another word for *very mean.*

crystal A *crystal* is a shiny material that has flat sides and sharp edges.

curious When you are *curious* about something, you want to know about that thing.

cute Something that is good-looking and charming is *cute.*

dart When things move very fast, they *dart.*

deadly fear A *deadly fear* is a great fear.

deathly If something reminds you of death, that thing is *deathly.*

decorate When you *decorate* something, you add things to make it look prettier.

dedicated If something is *dedicated* to a person, it is done out of respect to that person.

demand When you *demand* something, you insist on that thing.

Denali *Denali* is the name of a huge mountain in Alaska.

deserve Something you *deserve* is something you should receive.

disk A flat circle is a *disk.*

dragonflies *Dragonflies* are insects with wings that you can see through.

emergency brake An *emergency brake* is a brake you use if the regular brake does not work.

endurance *Endurance* tells how long you can keep doing something.

especially *Especially* is another word for *really.*

examination An *examination* is a checkup.

exchange *Exchange* is another word for *trade.*

exclaim When you *exclaim,* you say something as if it is very important.

experience Each thing you do is an *experience.*

extend When you *extend* something, you stretch it out.

familiar Things that are well-known to you are *familiar* to you.

fantastic Another word for *fantastic* is *wonderful.*

feat Amazing things that people do are *feats.*

fierce Something that is very wild is *fierce.*

flail When you *flail* your arms, you swing them around in all directions.

flop   If something is a *flop,* that thing did not work well.

folks   *Folks* is another word for *people.*

forearm   The *forearm* is the part of the arm that goes from the elbow to the wrist.

galaxy   A *galaxy* is a group of millions and millions of stars.

gear   The supplies and equipment that you take with you are called your *gear.*

gorilla   A *gorilla* is a huge member of the ape family.

grasp   If you *grasp* something, you grab it and hold on to it.

Greeley   *Greeley* is a city in Colorado.

guide   A *guide* is a person who shows the way.

gust   A *gust* of wind is a strong wind that starts suddenly and doesn't last long.

harnessed   When a sled-dog team is attached to a sled, the team is *harnessed* to the sled.

health   Your *health* refers to how well your body is.

hero   A *hero* is somebody we admire for having great courage or doing great things.

hip joint   The place where the leg joins the hip is the *hip joint.*

history   *History* is the study of the past.

horizon   The *horizon* is the line where the earth ends and the sky begins.

husky   A *husky* is a strong sled dog that survives well in very cold weather.

Iditarod   The *Iditarod* is a sled-dog race that is run every year in Alaska.

image   An *image* is a picture.

imagination   Your *imagination* is the part of your mind that can think of things that might happen.

include   When you *include* something, you let it inside something else.

indeed   *Indeed* is another word for *certainly.*

injured   *Injured* is another word for hurt.

injury   If a person has an *injury,* that person is seriously hurt.

insist   When you keep arguing that you must have something, you *insist* on that thing.

instructor   Another word for *teacher* is *instructor.*

intelligent   *Intelligent* is another word for *smart.*

iris   The *iris* of the eye is the part that is colored.

iron   *Iron* is a heavy metal that magnets stick to.

jammed   *Jammed* is another word for *crowded.*

kennel   A *kennel* is a place where dogs are kept.

Knik   *Knik* is the name of a town in Alaska.

lantern   A lamp that sends out light in all directions is a *lantern.*

leopard   A *leopard* is a member of the cat family that lives in Africa.

level   When something is *level,* it is flat.

limp   The opposite of *stiff* is *limp.*

lungs   Your *lungs* are the organs in your chest that you use when you breathe.

magnifying   Something that is *magnified* is made larger.

mass   A *mass* of things is a large number of those things crowded together.

midnight   *Midnight* is the middle of the night.

miserable   *Miserable* is another word for *terrible.*

mob   When people crowd around something, they *mob* that thing.

molecule   *Molecules* are the smallest parts of a material.

muscles   *Muscles* are attached to bones and move those bones so you can move.

musher   A *musher* is a person who drives a sled-dog team.

nerve   *Nerves* are like wires that carry messages to the brain and the body.

nightmare   A *nightmare* is a bad, bad dream.

Nome   *Nome* is a very small city in Alaska.

nonsense   *Nonsense* means *no sense at all.*

o'clock   *O'clock* tells about the hour of the day.

official An *official* is somebody who can judge if things are done as they are supposed to be done.

overcome When you *overcome* a problem, you solve it.

panic When you *panic,* you become so afraid that your mind doesn't work well.

paralyzed If a body part is *paralyzed,* it can't move.

parka A *parka* is a warm jacket with a hood.

partner A *partner* is somebody you do something with.

peer When you look at something as hard as you can, you *peer* at that thing.

permit When you let something happen, you *permit* it to happen.

Plateosaurus *Plateosaurus* was the very first dinosaur.

platform A *platform* is a level place that is above the places around it.

plunge If something *plunges* into the water, it dives into the water.

porpoise A *porpoise* is sometimes called a dolphin.

prevent When you *prevent* something, you make sure it doesn't happen.

protect When you *protect* something, you don't let anything hurt it.

prove When you *prove* something, you show that it has to be true.

pulse When something *pulses,* it beats.

purpose If you do something on *purpose,* you do something the way you planned to do it.

rapidly Another word for *quickly* is *rapidly.*

recently If something happened not long ago, that thing happened *recently.*

reef A *reef* is a ridge that forms underwater.

regular *Regular* is another word for *usual* or *ordinary.*

reins *Reins* are the straps that are attached to horses.

relax When you *relax,* you take it easy.

retina The *retina* is the part of the eye where pictures are formed.

Reading Mastery Plus **Level 4** Teacher's Guide **99**

saber   A *saber* is a kind of sword.

scene   If you look at something with many things or parts to it, you're looking at a *scene.*

scent   Another word for the *smell* of something is the *scent* of something.

science   The careful study of anything in the world is a *science.*

scuba diver   A *scuba diver* goes underwater wearing a mask and a tank of air.

separated   Things that are *separated* are no longer together.

sheltered   Things that are *sheltered* are protected.

shortly   Another word for *soon* is *shortly.*

single   *Single* means *one.*

skull   Your *skull* is the bone that covers the top of your head.

spinal cord   The *spinal cord* is the bundle of nerves that goes down the middle of your backbone.

spiral   A *spiral* is a circle that keeps getting bigger.

squid   A *squid* is a sea animal that looks like an octopus that has ten tentacles.

straining   When somebody pulls or pushes as hard as possible, the person is *straining.*

success   When you have *success,* you do very well at something.

surfaces   When a diver *surfaces,* the diver swims up to the surface of the water.

suspended   Things that are *suspended* are hung in space.

Sweden   *Sweden* is a country that's part of the land the Vikings once ruled.

swooping   When birds dip down and glide back up, they are *swooping.*

tarp   A *tarp* is a large covering made of canvas or plastic.

tempted   If you are *tempted* to do something, part of you wants to do it but another part doesn't.

tentacles   A squid's *tentacles* are its ten arms.

terrific   *Terrific* is another word for *wonderful.*

thorough   Something is *thorough* if it doesn't overlook anything.

tightrope   A *tightrope* is a rope high above the ground that circus people walk on.

tour   When you go on a *tour,* you take a trip to several places.

trails   If something *trails,* it follows behind something else.

transparent   If something is *transparent,* you can see things clearly through it.

triceps   The *triceps* is the muscle on the back of the upper arm.

troop   A *troop* is a group of baboons that are related.

trudge   When you *trudge,* you walk along slowly.

tune   A *tune* is a song.

twilight   *Twilight* is the time just after the sun goes down.

unbearable   If you can't stand something, that thing is *unbearable.*

universe   The *universe* is everything there is—all the galaxies and everything in them.

usual   Things that are *usual* are things that happen most of the time.

veld   The *veld* is a large open plain or field in Africa that goes for miles and miles.

veterinarian   A *veterinarian* is an animal doctor.

vibrate   When something *vibrates,* it moves back and forth so fast you can hardly see it move.

victory   Another word for a *win* is a *victory.*

visibility   *Visibility* is how well you can see things.

volunteer   A *volunteer* is a person who does a job without pay.

waste   When we *waste* something, we use it the wrong way.

weary   Another word for *very tired* is *weary.*

white-capped   A *white-capped* wave is a wave with white foam on top of it.

woman's   Something that belongs to a woman is the *woman's.*

wriggle   When something *wriggles,* it squirms and moves in all directions.

x-ray   An *x-ray* is a photograph that shows someone's bones.

yucky   Things that are unpleasant or foul or slimy are *yucky.*

aboard	56	armor	23
above	3	arrange	36
absolutely	129	arranged	37
according	93	arrangements	98
actually	15	aside	42
addressed	115	assigned	61
admission	73	assignment	39
adult	55	assistant	93
adults	56	assistants	94
adventure	32	Atlantic Ocean	23
Africa	23	attaching	64
agreeing	101	attorney	45
agreement	51	attract	31
aha	132	attracting	69
aimed	58	attractive	131
aimlessly	99	audience	67
aisle	57	automatic	46
alarm	94	automatically	38
Alaskan	12	automobile	35
alongside	91	avoid	82
aloud	27	award	99
amused	95	baboon	131
Anchorage	88	backbone	125
anchored	86	backwards	93
Anderson	139	backyard	69
Andros Island	23	badly	85
Angela	99	baggage	56
angrily	76	bailing	26
announcer	46	bakery	41
answering	68	balanced	116
answers	2	bald	49
anxious	99	bandage	34
anxiously	114	bandages	35
anymore	3	bare	82
anyone	28	barks	137
anytime	138	barns	4
anywhere	101	barracuda	87
appear	52	basketball	47
appeared	58	bathroom	44
applaud	68	bathrooms	59
applauded	74	bathtub	41
applause	48	beak	74
approach	34	beam	42
approached	35	bedroom	126
area	59	bedtime	41
argument	89	below	5
arithmetic	39	bending	28

beneath	34	buzzer	41
Bermuda Triangle	23	cabinet	57
besides	26	cage	69
beware	97	camera	132
biceps	116	camp	134
billion	105	canvas	92
birthday	96	carefully	109
blind	125	careless	15
blinding	27	Carla	24
blisters	34	carrot	75
blizzard	94	ceiling	37
blocking	42	cell	122
blood vessel	121	cerebrum	123
blush	108	certainly	54
boarded	56	certificate	93
boat-shaped	123	certificates	94
bodies	89	challenging	94
booklet	52	chamber	121
bookstore	138	changing	77
booming	45	chant	75
booties	92	character	35
boss	49	charges	47
bow	26	checker	39
Bowman	96	checkered	56
brain	87	checkpoint	94
branched	87	chest	1
barracuda		chew	34
bravery	84	child	85
breakfast	57	chilly	101
breath	29	choked	37
breathe	32	choose	119
breaths	31	chosen	52
breeze	2	Christmas	81
brightest	118	chuckled	38
brightly	58	Chugger	94
briskly	128	circles	4
broadly	111	circling	59
bubbling	62	Clarks Hill Lake	8
buddies	99	classroom	55
bundle	125	claws	84
buoyancy	88	clean	66
buoyancy device	87	cleaning	69
buoyant	87	clearer	43
burner	105	clearing	29
business	46	clever	42
businesslike	49	cliff	15
butterflies	63	closest	129

close-up 62	cruel 96	disk 114	Eskimo 11
cloth 47	crunchy 62	display 36	especially 87
clothing 56	crust 98	disturb 67	Esther 36
cloudy 08	crystal 105	dived 3	events 95
club 29	crystals 106	divided 33	evergreen 96
collar 39	curb 134	doctor 56	everybody 129
collect 125	curious 99	dome 61	everyone 36
collects 127	current 17	doorbell 134	examination 89
comfortable 53	curved 133	doorknob 107	examined 93
command 89	curvy 132	dove 21	example 41
commands 91	cute 68	dragonflies 138	excellent 48
comment 131	dance 42	drawings 43	exchange 93
commented 132	dangerous 13	dressing 128	exciting 24
company 45	dangers 5	drew 44	exclaimed 114
compass 97	darkness 57	dried 98	excuse 42
competed 95	Darla 85	driven 28	exercise 58
complained 58	darted 36	drowned 18	exercises 59
completed 58	darting 87	drums 44	exhibit 35
computer 57	day-dreaming 54	during 48	expect 42
concluded 51	daylight 9	dust 69	expensive 115
confidence 82	daytime 5	eagle 31	experience 73
confused 5	deadly fear 85	earlier 22	explained 127
congratulate 98	deathly 84	earliest 23	explaining 23
congratulated 99	December 11	earmuffs 41	explanation 38
connected 46	deciding 49	earn 66	explodes 33
constant 9	decorated 118	earrings 84	explosion 33
contacted 78	decorations 132	Edna Parker 24	expression 36
control 106	dedicated 94	eighteen 54	extend 136
conversation 82	deliver 68	elbow 49	extends 137
cookbook 138	delivering 69	electrical 45	eyeball 126
coral 87	demand 99	electricity 36	failure 55
correct 129	demanded 101	elephants 67	faint 28
correctly 54	demanding 95	elevator 25	fainted 67
cost 47	demonstrate 57	eleven 49	familiar 101
couch 116	demonstrated 77	eleventh 56	fancy 52
cough 32	demonstrating 121	embarrassed 35	fantastic 73
coughed 37	Denali 89	emergency 83	fastened 57
coughing 33	dents 19	emergency brake 82	feat 95
counter 42	deserve 71	empty 39	February 11
couple 78	deserves 72	Endurance 133	female 1
courage 94	device 41	endurance 93	fewer 7
cover 53	diagram 45	enemies 136	fierce 94
crackle 62	diagrams 46	energy 41	figure 22
crackling 102	difference 119	engineer 23	film 62
crater 62	differently 122	enjoying 66	final 53
crazier 36	difficult 41	enter 15	finisher 99
creaks 16	dimmed 51	entered 87	fired 119
create 108	dimmer 114	entering 44	first mate 25
created 111	dinosaur 22	equator 3	flailed 86
creepy 101	dipped 71	equipment 54	flaming 117
crept 134	directed 33	equipped 61	flapping 1
crisp 91	directing 84	era 138	flatly 51
crooked 6	disappointed 46	erasing 129	flat-topped 137
crowded 28	discussed 127	erupting 59	fliers 2

Reading Word List

lightning 26	mobbed 69	one-way 44	pickup 82
limp 94	model 46	Oolak 12	pigeon 66
liquid 57	molecule 105	Oomoo 12	pigeons 67
locker 89	mommy 72	opening 71	pinched 89
lonely 1	Monday 35	operator 48	pink 121
loudspeaker 47	monster 31	ordinary 11	pinwheel 118
lowest 75	months 1	outdoors 37	pirates 25
lumpy 114	mosquito 15	outfit 43	planet 53
lungs 121	mosquitoes 16	outing 36	plastic 41
lying 31	mouthful 31	outside 58	Plateosaurus 136
magazine 36	mouthpiece 86	overboard 35	platform 82
magnetic 53	Mr. Martin 95	overcome 89	playful 13
magnifying 123	Mrs. Wilson 85	overhang 62	playfully 19
mailman 126	Ms. Siri Carlson 96	overturned 28	playmate 13
male 1	muddy 39	owe 46	plunge 97
manage 63	mukluks 21	owed 21	plunged 98
managed 64	muscle 115	owner 69	Pluto 52
manufacturer 46	muscles 117	oxygen 55	polar bear 12
manufacturers 47	museum 35	pace 36	policemen 83
marble 19	mushed 95	Pacific Ocean 52	police officer 84
March 11	musher 89	pacing 32	pond 29
Maria Sanchez 71	music 72	package 116	ponds 1
markings 1	myself 37	packages 138	popcorn 107
married 89	mysterious 34	packed 56	porpoise 134
Mars 53	narrow 103	packing 32	possible 35
masks 69	neck 5	pages 138	pour 32
mass 87	neither 32	pair 87	pours 33
masses 125	Neptune 52	pale 65	powered 25
mast 25	nerve 124	palms 57	practice 26
matching 41	nervous 53	pancakes 139	practiced 29
material 36	Newmans Lake 9	panic 85	practicing 43
maybe 126	next-smartest 137	panicked 86	praised 48
meals 66	nicer 16	paralyzed 121	prancing 32
meantime 47	nightmare 93	parents 52	prepare 66
mentioned 41	nighttime 129	parka 91	presented 116
meow 66	nodding 129	parrot 66	pressed 82
meowed 71	Nome 89	parrots 67	pressure 55
Mercury 52	nonsense 111	partly 57	pretend 25
merry 139	nor 34	partner 85	prettiest 118
Mesozoic 22	no-see-ums 15	party 134	prevent 132
mess 39	notebook 47	patent 45	prevents 133
message 54	notebooks 48	paused 49	prize 47
Michael 66	nowhere 117	pebbled 12	products 49
Michigan 6	nudged 14	pecked 75	program 61
midnight 101	numb 16	pedal 39	protect 119
migrate 1	observed 102	peered 97	protection 38
migration 1	observer 111	pencils 36	prove 111
Milky Way 118	o'clock 72	peppy 73	provided 56
million 52	offer 51	perfectly 79	puddle 103
miserable 94	office 54	perhaps 26	pulse 124
mistakes 129	officer 81	permission 45	punish 15
mitten 131	official 92	permit 121	punishment 16
mixed 123	officials 93	pest 93	pupil 126
moaned 27	older 7	photo 95	puppies 72

purchase 45	Rita 39	sharply 83	solve 67
purple 64	river 7	sharp-minded 37	somehow 27
purpose 91	rivers 6	she'd 42	somersault 72
purred 71	rocket 103	sheltered 98	somersaults 73
pyramid 77	rocketing 58	shocked 114	son 11
quake 33	rose 21	shocks 124	song 74
questioned 56	roughed 25	shoelace 124	soup 61
quick 135	route 4	shopkeeper 41	sour 43
quit 86	sabers 135	shorter 1	South Carolina 9
rabbit 138	safety 32	shortly 76	spaceship 53
racer 102	sailed 31	shoulder 12	spaceships 138
racetrack 102	Samson 62	shovel 125	spaghetti 66
railroad 37	sandwiches 35	shower 58	spear 11
rainy 96	San Francisco 52	showers 59	speckled 15
raise 41	Sarah 39	shown 8	speech 36
rapidly 86	Saturn 53	shrank 16	speeded 102
rapped 45	scariest 64	shriek 29	speedometer 102
reaches 9	scattered 12	sidewalk 74	spelling 112
ready 66	scene 86	sideways 58	spinal 121
realized 109	scent 96	Sidney 55	spinal cord 122
realizing 43	schoolwork 81	sighed 45	spiral 125
reason 32	schoolyard 16	sight 21	splashing 9
reasons 49	science 102	silent 25	splat 13
receive 4	scientist 11	silently 117	splatter 12
receives 5	scientists 15	simply 104	splattered 62
recently 96	scooped 132	single 126	spoke 79
red-hot 63	score 53	sipped 65	spoon 71
Reedy Lake 7	Scott 134	sir 9	spoonful 117
reef 85	scrambled 14	sissy 85	spotlight 49
referring 91	scratched 116	skeleton 22	sprang 5
refund 76	screech 69	skull 121	spread 29
regular 78	screeching 67	sleeve 96	spun 134
reins 91	screen 136	sliced 15	spyglass 25
relax 106	screw 84	slices 135	square 132
remained 51	scuba 85	slid 31	squawking 24
remains 32	seagulls 25	sloshed 26	squid 113
remembering 56	season 8	sloshing 15	squirrel 66
remind 49	secret 45	slowpoke 13	squirting 115
reminded 74	section 53	slumped 64	stack 138
repeated 13	select 1	smoked 64	stage 49
replace 94	selected 53	smoking 47	stairway 37
report 52	sense 29	snack 54	stared 129
resold 78	separated 86	snappy 45	staring 104
respond 41	serious 66	snored 59	started 31
restless 11	serves 42	snowball 13	steam 29
retina 125	serving 59	snowdrift 13	steering 82
retrained 78	seventeen 72	snowdrifts 14	stern 25
returned 78	seventy 9	snowflake 118	sternly 41
reward 72	shadow 34	snowmobile 96	stiff 87
rewarded 73	shaft 44	snowstorm 134	stiffen 92
rice 71	shallow 26	soda 87	stiffened 93
ridge 14	shame 45	softly 76	stinging 96
ridiculous 66	shapes 64	solar system 52	stings 124
rim 34	sharper 6	solution 39	stinks 43

stir 101	tea 65	trout 5	volunteers 96
stomach 34	tearing 26	trucks 67	wagging 69
stormy 24	teasing 88	trudged 96	waist 57
stove 74	telescope 61	tube 121	Waldo Greem 67
strain 91	telescopes 62	tucking 98	wallet 135
strained 92	temperature 108	Tuesday 34	walrus 12
strangely 32	tempted 96	tumbling 14	walruses 13
strangest 28	tentacles 113	tune 74	wandering 48
streak 54	terrible 28	turner-off-er 46	warned 62
stream 29	terribly 29	twelve 54	warning 24
strings 63	terrific 139	twenty-five 53	waste 77
striped 59	Terry 65	twilight 87	watermelon 114
strongest 131	thermometer 129	tying 126	wavy 21
struck 96	thick 29	typed 136	weary 95
struggling 88	thicker 119	Tyrannosaurus 22	we'll 59
student 51	thirty 54	ugh 121	we're 59
studied 112	thorough 89	unbearable 112	weightless 57
stuffed 37	throat 34	Uncle Chad 91	welcome 56
stumbled 27	throughout 129	uncovered 54	well 59
stung 18	thud 33	underlined 55	Wendy 52
subtract 39	thumb 122	understand 37	were 59
success 81	thunder 27	understood 82	whenever 41
sudden 2	tightrope 73	underwater 33	whether 44
suffer 88	tilted 9	unfastened 58	whew 69
suggest 38	tingles 63	unfolded 41	whistled 79
suggested 39	tiptoe 25	unfrozen 4	white-capped 89
suit 56	tiptoed 26	unhappy 84	whoa 91
suitcase 62	tires 82	unimportant 117	winding 82
summertime 131	titled 133	universe 116	wintertime 9
supper 43	Tokyo 55	unpacked 62	woman's 81
supplies 32	tone 43	unreal 34	wool 91
supply 46	toothbrush 56	untangle 32	wore 69
suppose 52	tossing 14	unties 95	workout 58
surface 17	total 97	unusually 71	world's 67
surfaced 85	touch 25	upright 28	worried 54
surprise 99	toughness 91	upside 58	wriggled 113
surprised 101	tour 73	upside-down 79	wrist 21
surround 59	tours 81	upstairs 76	written 53
surrounded 61	towels 39	upwards 88	x-ray 94
survive 57	towers 61	Uranus 52	yapping 91
Susie 91	traced 42	Usk 13	yeah 66
suspended 129	traded 89	usual 111	yearly 1
swallow 63	trail 29	vehicle 63	yesterday 35
swarming 15	trailed 87	Velcro 92	you'd 74
sweater 134	trailer 81	veld 131	young 51
sweaters 135	trainer 67	Venus 53	yucky 72
Sweden 95	training 3	veterinarian 89	zebra 66
swift 33	transparent 115	vibrate 108	zebras 67
swooping 102	traveler 54	vibrating 109	zero 91
tail 29	tremble 57	victory 99	zipped 62
tangle 28	triangle 6	view 59	zoo 67
tank 58	triceps 115	visibility 94	zoomed 118
target 42	Triceratops 22	vocabulary 38	
tarps 98	trickles 124	volcano 32	
taught 72	troops 131	volunteer 95	

APPENDIX F—READING SELECTIONS

LESSON NUMBER	COMPREHENSION PASSAGE	MAIN STORY TITLE
1	Facts About Geese	Old Henry
2	More Facts About Geese	Henry Meets Tim
3	Directions on Maps	Tim's Questions
4	Facts About the Earth	Tim Has a Flying Lesson
5	Facts About the Equator	Tim Practices Flying
6	The Sun Lights the Earth	The Geese Leave Big Trout Lake
7	Michigan and Kentucky	Old Henry Tests Tim
8	The Sun Heats the Earth	A New Plan
9	The Sun and the Earth	Flying With the Flock
11	The Tilt of the Earth	The Flock Reaches Florida
12	Facts About Eskimos	Back to Canada
13	1) Animals in Alaska 2) Where Oomoo and Oolak Lived	Oomoo
14	The Dangerous Season	Usk, The Polar Bear
15	Florida, Canada and Alaska	Playing with Usk
16	Facts About Killer Whales	The Beach
17		The Ice Floe
18	Facts About Drifting	Drifting on an Ice Chunk
19		The Storm
21	Facts About Clouds	The Killer Whales Wait
22	Piles	Usk and the Killer Whale
23		Layers of the Earth
24	Dinosaurs of the Mesozoic	Edna Parker
25		Looking for Something to Do
26		The Lifeboat
27	Facts About Whirlpools	A Giant Whirlpool
28		A Long Night
29		Footprints
31		The Monster
32		Looking for Carla
33	Volcanos and Earthquakes	Explosion
34	Underlined Words	Back in the Lifeboat
35		Saved
36	Inventing	Grandmother Esther
37		Grandmother Esther's Inventions
38		Trying to Discover Needs
39		Bad Ideas
41		A Plan for Inventing
42		The Electric Eye
43		A Good Idea
44		One Way
45		Another Problem
46		Leonard's Model
47		An Invention Fair
48		The Manufacturers at the Fair
49		Deals

LESSON NUMBER	COMPREHENSION PASSAGE	MAIN STORY TITLE
51		The First-Prize Winner
52	Facts About Japan	Your Turn
53	Facts About the Solar System	An Important Test
54	Past, Present and Future	The Test Questions
55		Waiting for a Letter
56	More About Japan	A Surprise at the Space Station
57		Traveler Four
58	Gravity	The Gravity Device
59		Jupiter
61		Io
62	Planets and Gravity	The Space Station on Io
63		A Trip to the Volcano
64		Help
65		Sidney
66		Back to Earth
67	Kinds of Animals	Waldo's Cooking
68		A Problem
69	Training Animals	Waldo Gets a Job
71	Teaching Animals a Hard Trick	The Pet Shop
72		Maria and Waldo Make a Deal
73		Waldo Starts Training Animals
74		The Animal Show
75		A Big Crowd
76		Problems at the Pet Shop
77		Changing the Rewards
78		New Rewards and a New Super Trick
79	Colorado and Utah	A Great Show
81		Plans for a Trip
82		On the Tour
83		The Pyramid
84	Facts About Coral	The Animals' Greatest Show
85		Darla's Fear
86	Facts About Pressure	Getting Ready to Dive
87		An Underwater World
88		An Emergency
89		The Trip to the Water's Surface
91	Sled-Dog Teams	Susie and Denali
92	Booties	Getting Ready for a Run
93		A Practice Run
94		Examination Day
95	Supplies for the Race	The Big Race
96	Checkpoints	On the Trail
97		Lost
98	Rest Periods	Beware of Streams
99		End of the Race

LESSON NUMBER	COMPREHENSION PASSAGE	MAIN STORY TITLE
101		Go Anywhere—See Anything
102	*The Speed of Light*	The First Trip
103		Al Learns More About Speed
104		Al Takes a Test About Speed
105		Al Learns About Matter
106		Al Visits Saturn and Pluto
107		Al Takes a Test on Matter
108		Al Takes Another Test
109		Al Learns About Molecules
111		Al Learns More About Molecules
112		Al Takes a Test About Molecules
113		Angela Meets the Old Man
114		Al and Angela Learn About Water Pressure
115		Al and Angela See Strange Sea Animals
116		Al and Angela Go to the Bottom of the Ocean
117		A Test About the Ocean
118		Angela and Al See Our Galaxy
119		Angela and Al Learn About Muscles
121		Al and Angela Learn About Bones
122		Angela and Al Learn About the Heart
123		Al and Angela Follow Blood Through the Body
124		Angela and Al Learn About Nerves
125	*Making Pictures With a Magnifying Glass*	Al and Angela Learn About the Brain
126	*How the Eye Works*	Al and Angela Learn About the Eye
127		Al and Angela Learn About the Ear
128		Al and Angela Study for a Test
129	*The Earth and the Sun*	Angela and Al Take a Test on the Human Body
131		Winter at the North Pole
132		Al and Angela Learn About Snowflakes
133	*The Camera and the Eye*	A Trip to the South Pole
134		A Book About the Poles
135	*Animals*	Al and Angela Buy Christmas Presents
136		Angela and Al Go to the Library
137		Angela and Al Read About Baboons
138		Al and Angela Finish Their Last Trip
139		Go Anywhere—See Anything With Books

Guide to Reproducible Appendices

Appendix A

Placement Test 82

Appendix G

Fact Games 112

(Reproduce 1 set for each group.)

Fact Game 10	*Fact Game 20*
Fact Game 30	*Fact Game 40*
Fact Game 50	*Fact Game 60*
Fact Game 70	*Fact Game 80*
Fact Game 90	*Fact Game 100*
Fact Game 110	*Fact Game 120*
Fact Game 130	*Fact Game 140*

Fact Game Scorecards 146

(Reproduce 1 of each sheet for each student.)

Appendix H

Group Summary Charts 148

(Reproduce 1 group sheet for every 10 lessons.)

Appendix I

Test Summary Sheets 150

(Reproduce 1 sheet for each 8 or fewer students in each group.)

Tests 1–7   *Tests 8–14*

Appendix J

Thermometer Charts 152

(Reproduce 1 of each sheet for each student.)

Appendix K

Map for Special Project
   After Lesson 10 154

Appendix L

Family Letters 155

Appendix O

Skills Profile Chart 181

2. a. Which line starts at the circle on the map and goes east?

    b. If you start at the circle and move to the number **3,** in which direction do you go?

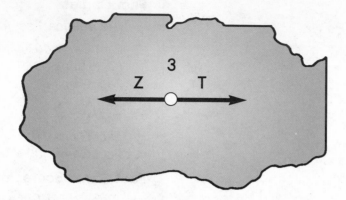

3. Tell which place is:

    a. the coldest

    b. the hottest

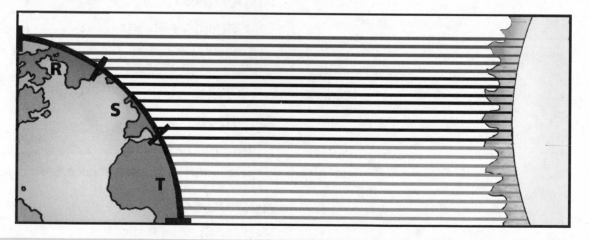

10

4. Which letter on the map shows Henry's landing place:

   a. in Florida?

   b. in Kentucky?

5. Which letter on the map shows Henry's landing place:

   a. in Canada?

   b. in Michigan?

6. Which letter on the map shows:

   a. Big Trout Lake?

   b. Crooked Lake?

   c. the first landing place?

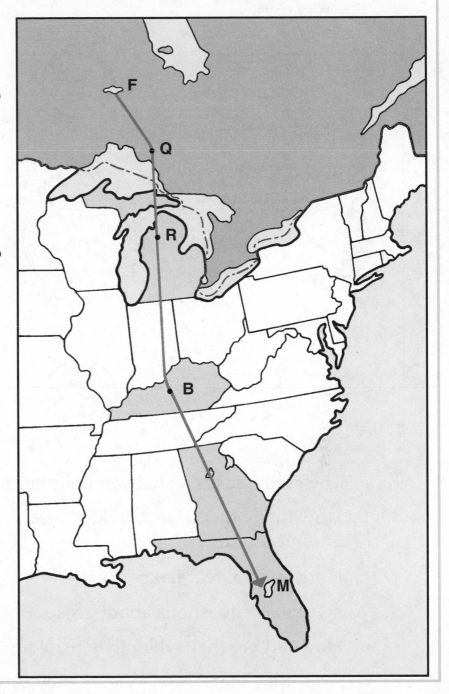

7. As you touch each Earth, say the letter. Then tell which season the Earth shows.

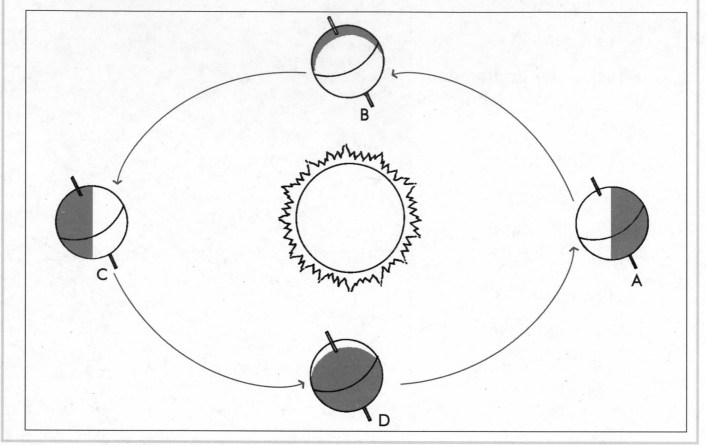

8. a. The earth makes a circle around the sun one time every ███.

   b. How many days does it take the earth to make one full circle around the sun?

   c. How many Great Lakes are there?

9. Answer these questions about geese:

   a. How old are they when they mate for the first time?

   b. After they mate, how long do they stay together?

   c. How long do most of them live?

10. In which direction do geese migrate:

   a. in the fall?

   b. in the spring?

11. a. Which side of Earth 1 is closer to the sun, **X** or **Y?**

b. Which side of Earth 1 is in daytime?

c. Which side of Earth 2 is in daytime?

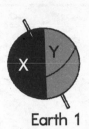

Earth 1

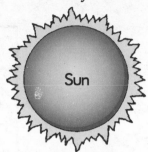

Sun

Earth 2

12. Which earth shows the person:

a. In daytime?

b. 6 hours later?

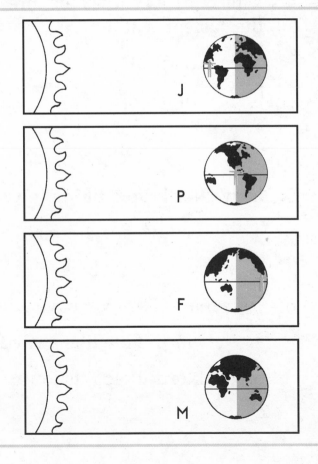

2. Tell which season each thing happens.

   a. Alaskan animals are the most dangerous.

   b. Female animals in Alaska have babies.

3. Which direction is:

   a. ocean current **F** moving?

   b. ocean current **J** moving?

   c. the wind coming from?

4. Which arrow shows the direction the current will move:

   a. ice chunk **B?**

   b. ice chunk **R?**

5. Is the North Pole tilting **toward the sun** or **away from the sun:**

   a. when days get shorter?

   b. when days get longer?

6. Tell what season we have when:

   a. the North Pole tilts **away from** the sun.

   b. the North Pole tilts **toward** the sun.

7. Which globe shows how the earth looks on the first day of:

   a. summer?

   b. winter?

G

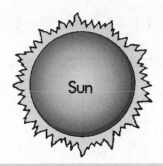

Sun

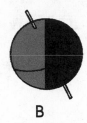

B

8. Which letter on the map shows:

   a. Canada?

   b. Alaska?

9. a. Which letter on the map shows the main part of the United States?

   b. Which **2** letters show where Eskimos live?

10. a. Name **3** cold-blooded animals.

    b. Name **3** warm-blooded animals.

11. a. Are killer whales fish?

    b. Are killer whales **cold-blooded** or **warm-blooded?**

12. a. How warm is it during winter in Alaska?

    b. In April, the sun shines for more than ▮▮▮ hours each day in Alaska.

2. Tell which footprint was made by:

   a. the lightest animal.

   b. the heaviest animal.

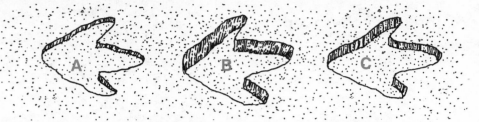

3. a. Whirlpools are made up of moving ▇▇▇.

   b. A whirlpool is shaped like a ▇▇▇.

4. Which came **later** on Earth:

   a. dinosaurs or strange sea animals?

   b. dinosaurs or horses?

5. Which layer went into the pile **later:**

   a. Layer C or layer A?

   b. Layer C or layer D?

6. Tell the letter of the layer that went into the pile:

   a. first

   b. next

   c. last

7. a. Tell the letter of the layer we live in.

   b. What's the name of layer **C?**

8. Tell the letter of the layer where we find:

   a. human skeletons

   b. horse skeletons

   c. dinosaur skeletons

9. As you touch each dinosaur, say the letter. Then tell the name of the dinosaur.

Fact Game

10. a. What kind of animals lived in the Mesozoic?

b. Things closest to the bottom of the pile went into the pile 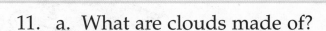.

11. a. What are clouds made of?

b. What kind of cloud does picture **C** show?

A   B   C

12. Tell the letters of the things you find in the Bermuda Triangle.

A. sudden storms   D. huge waves

B. streams   E. whirlpools

C. mountains   F. ice floes

2. Which object went into the pile:

   a. first?

   b. last?

3. Which object went into the pile **later:**

   a. the book or the rock?

   b. the bone or the cup?

4. Each picture has **2** arrows that show how the melted rock moves. Which picture shows **2** correct arrows?

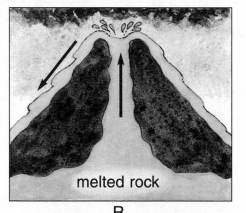

melted rock

R

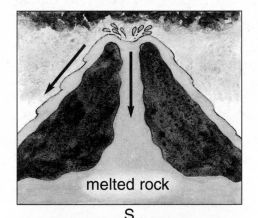

melted rock

S

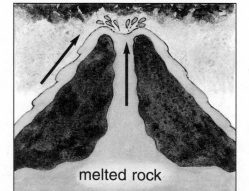

melted rock

T

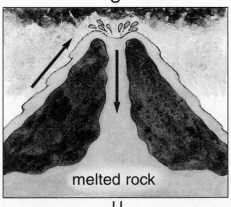

melted rock

U

5. Most of the things that we use every day were invented after the year ▆▆▆.

6. Which things were invented by somebody?

    trees   shoes   dirt

    pens   snow   flowers

    paper   grass   stoves

    rain   houses   cows

7. a. The person who makes an object for the first time is an ▆▆▆.

   b. The object the person makes is an ▆▆▆.

8. a. The first thing you do when you think like an inventor is find a ▆▆▆.

   b. What's the next thing you do?

9. The men who invented the airplane saw a need. What need?

10. How long ago did the dinosaurs live on Earth?

11. What is it called when the earth shakes and cracks?

12. Name **2** things that happen when melted rock moves down the sides of a volcano.

2. Answer these questions about Leonard's invention:

   a. How many electric eyes did he use?

   b. How many beams of light went across the doorway?

3. Answer these questions about Leonard's invention. Tell whether the person is moving **into the room** or **out of the room:**

   a. if the **outside** beam is broken first.

   b. if the **inside** beam is broken first.

4. As you touch each picture, say the letter. Then tell if the lights in the room are **on** or **off.**

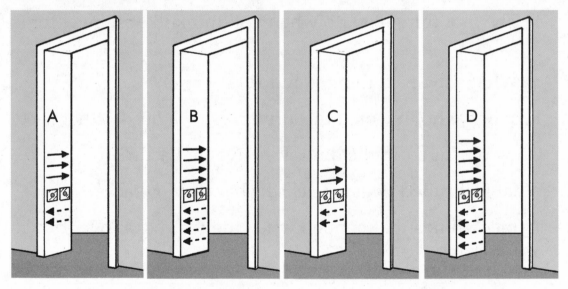

5. a. When you invent something, you start with a ▮▮▮▮.

   b. Then you build a ▮▮▮▮ of the invention.

   c. Then you get a ▮▮▮▮ to protect your invention.

6. What are businesses that make things called?

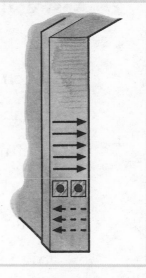

7. The solid arrows show how many people went into the room. The dotted arrows show how many people left the room.

    a. Are the lights on in the room?

    b. How many more people would have to leave the room before the lights go off?

8. a. What does an inventor get to protect an invention?

    b. Special lawyers who get protection for inventions are called .

9. Tell what the counter on Leonard's device does:

    a. every time somebody goes into the room.

    b. every time somebody leaves the room.

10. Answer these questions about Leonard's invention:

    a. If a person moves **into** the room, which beam is broken first— the inside beam or the outside beam?

    b. Which beam is broken next?

    c. Will the lights turn **on** or **off?**

11. Here's the rule about an electric eye: **Each time the beam of light is broken, the light changes.** For each item, tell if the light is **on** or **off** at the end.

    a. The light is off. The beam is broken 4 times.

    b. The light is off. The beam is broken 3 times.

12. a. What number does Leonard's counter end up at when the last person leaves the room?

    b. What happens to the lights?

2. Answer these questions about Earth and Mars:

   a. Which is **smaller?**

   b. Which has **more** clouds around it?

   c. Which is **warmer?**

3. If something weighed 100 pounds on Earth:

   a. would it weigh more than 100 pounds on Saturn?

   b. would it weigh more than 100 pounds on our moon?

   c. how much would it weigh on our moon?

4. a. How far is it from Earth to Jupiter?

   b. Which is smaller, Earth or Saturn?

5. A person weighs 100 pounds on planet X and 200 pounds on planet Y. Which planet has stronger gravity?

6. a. Is Earth the planet that is closest to the sun?

   b. The sun gives ████ and ████ to all the planets.

7. a. What's in the middle of the solar system?

   b. Name the planet we live on.

   c. Name the only part of the solar system that's burning.

8. Tell how many moons each planet has.

   a. Saturn

   b. Jupiter

9. Say all the planets in the solar system. Mercury, ████, ████, Mars, ████, Saturn, ████, Neptune, ████.

10. a. Which planet is largest?

     b. Which planet is next-largest?

     c. How many times larger than Earth is the sun?

11. Tell how many:

     a. planets are in the solar system.

     b. suns are in the solar system.

12. a. Which is bigger, Alaska or Japan?

     b. Is Japan a **state** or a **country?**

     c. What's the largest city in Japan?

2. What's another name for hot, melted rock?

3. As you touch animals **A, B** and **C,** say the letter. Then name the animal.

4. As you touch animals **D, E** and **F,** say the letter. Then name the animal.

5. a. How long does it take Jupiter to spin around one time?

   b. Which uses more oxygen, running or sitting?

6. Answer these questions about Jupiter and Io:

   a. Which has **stronger** gravity?

   b. Which is **smaller** than Earth?

   c. Where can you jump 8 feet high?

7. a. Does Io move around Jupiter **slowly** or **fast?**

    b. It takes Io about ▬▬▬ to go all the way around Jupiter.

8. When you're training an animal, what do you do:

    a. each time the animal does the trick?

    b. if the animal does not do the trick?

9. a. Which has **stronger** gravity—Earth or Jupiter?

    b. So where would you feel **lighter?**

10. What color is lava:

    a. when it's very hot?

    b. when it's completely cooled?

11. a. Do gases surround Io?

    b. How much oxygen is on Io?

12. a. What planet is shown in the picture?

    b. Which is bigger, the "eye" of the planet or Earth?

2. Say **top** or **bottom** for each blank.

   a. A regular pyramid has one animal at the ▇▇ of the pyramid.

   b. An upside-down pyramid has one animal at the ▇▇ of the pyramid.

3. Tell the letter of the glass that will make:

   a. the lowest ring.

   b. the highest ring.

4. a. Name 2 cities in Colorado.

   b. Name one city in Utah.

5. Tell about driving from Colorado to Utah.

   a. What mountains do you drive over?

   b. In which direction do you go?

6. a. When you teach an animal to work for a new reward, do you change the reward **quickly** or **slowly?**

   b. When do you stop changing the reward?

7. When you teach an animal a simple trick:

   a. when do you reward the animal?

   b. when don't you reward the animal?

8. a. When you teach an animal to work for a new reward, what kind of reward do you start with?

   b. Then what do you do to that reward?

9. As you touch **A** and **B**, say the letter. Then name the state.

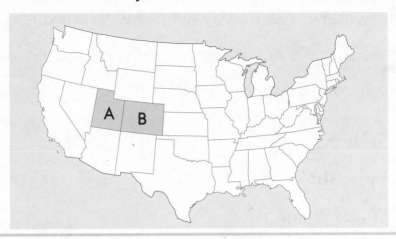

10. The more water the glass has, the ▮▮▮▮ the sound it makes.

    • higher   • lower

11. When you're teaching a hard trick:

    a. can the animal do the trick at first?

    b. what happens if the animal doesn't receive rewards until it does the trick?

    c. what do you reward the animal for doing at first?

12. A person weighs 200 pounds on planet X and 100 pounds on planet Y. Which planet has stronger gravity?

2. a. Coral is made up of tiny ███.

 b. An underwater ridge that's covered with coral is called a coral ███.

3. a. What does the color of water tell you about the water?

 b. Name an arrow-shaped fish.

4. Tell which body has:

 a. the most pressure on it?

 b. the least pressure on it?

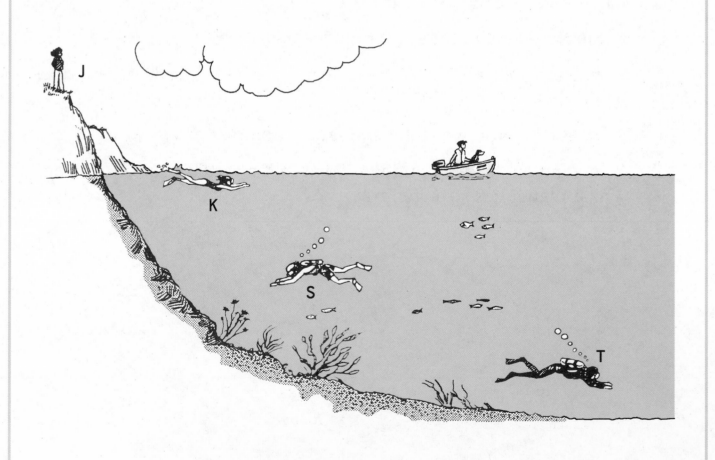

5. a. When you open a bottle of soda pop, what happens to the pressure inside the bottle?

    b. What forms in the soda pop?

6. a. In what ocean is the **X?**

    b. About how many miles is it from Florida to the **X?**

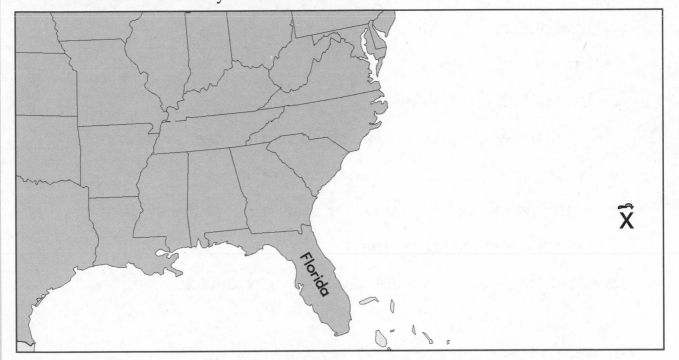

7. How many times greater is the pressure on you:

    a. when you dive down 33 feet?

    b. when you dive down 66 feet?

8. When you move up too fast from very deep water:

    a. you may get the ████.

    b. what forms in your blood?

    c. is there **less pressure** or **more pressure** on your body?

Fact Game

9. a. The Iditarod is about ▮▮▮▮ miles from start to finish.

       • 2000   • 200   • 1100

  b. In most years, the race takes about ▮▮▮▮.

       • 3 days   • 10 days   • 3 weeks

10. Answer these questions about the Iditarod sled-dog race.

  a. In what state is it held?

  b. In what city does it begin?

  c. In what city does it end?

11. Answer these questions about the ocean 100 feet down.

  a. Is the water all the same temperature?

  b. Is the water **cooler** or **warmer** than water at the surface?

  c. Do things look **light** or **dark?**

12. Answer these questions about a buoyancy device.

  a. What is it filled with?

  b. When it is filled up, what happens to the diver?

  c. When it is empty, what happens to the diver?

100

Fact Game

2. Tell what could happen if booties on a sled dog are:

   a. too loose.

   b. too tight.

3. a. Most sled-dog teams have an ▮▮▮ number of dogs.

      • even   • odd

   b. For the Iditarod, a sled-dog team can't have more than ▮▮▮ dogs.

4. Answer these questions about Iditarod rules.

   a. What does a musher have to do with an injured dog?

   b. At least how many dogs must be on the gang line at the end of the race?

   c. Every musher must rest for ▮▮▮ hours at one checkpoint and for ▮▮▮ hours at 2 other checkpoints.

5. a. Name the first woman who won the Iditarod.

   b. In what year did she win it?

6. Answer these questions about the Iditarod.

   a. How much food does each dog need every day?

      • 1 pound   • 2 pounds   • 5 pounds

   b. Each sled must have room to hold ▮▮▮.

      • an injured musher

      • an injured dog

      • 100 pounds of food

7. Say which dogs each item tells about:

      • wheel dogs   • swing dogs   • lead dogs

   a. Which dogs are responsible for freeing the sled when it gets stuck?

   b. Which dogs are very smart and do other dogs obey?

   c. Which dogs are very good followers and smart?

Appendix G Lesson 100—Fact Game **135**

8. What command tells sled dogs:

    a. to turn left?

    b. to turn right?

    c. to move straight ahead?

9. a. Name the woman who finished the Iditarod 16 times.

    b. How many times did she enter the Iditarod?

    c. How many times did she finish in first place?

10. Tell which things each Iditarod musher must have.

    - enough food for a week
    - enough food for a day
    - a good sleeping bag
    - extra shoes
    - firewood
    - booties
    - an ax
    - a tent
    - extra dogs
    - snowshoes

11. Answer these questions about Iditarod checkpoints.

    a. How does food get to them?

    b. About how far apart are they?

    c. About how many are there?

12. Answer these questions about Iditarod rules.

    a. What happens if a sled dog doesn't pass the health examination?

    b. How much help can mushers get when they're on the trail?

2. a. What are tiny parts of matter called?

    b. How many forms of matter are there?

3. In what form of matter is air:

    a. on Earth?

    b. on Pluto?

    c. on Saturn?

4. How can you change:

    a. solid matter into liquid matter?

    b. gas matter into liquid matter?

5. What form of matter is:

    a. the air around you?

    b. the sun?

6. a. How many miles does light travel in one second?

    b. What else travels as fast as light?

7. Tell how long it takes:

    a. sound to travel one mile.

    b. light to travel from the sun to Earth.

8. Name all the things in the list below that are matter in the solid form.

    - air
    - water
    - milk
    - steam
    - wood
    - rock
    - tea
    - glass

9. Name all the things in the list above that are matter in the gas form.

10. Tell which thing in the list below:

   a. travels fastest.

   b. travels slowest.

   - racing car
   - sound
   - rocket
   - light
   - jet plane

11. What form of matter is:

   a. water?

   b. ice?

   c. steam?

12. Name each form of matter:

   a. the coldest form

   b. the next-coldest form

   c. the hottest form

Fact Game

2. a. In which form of matter are molecules lined up in rows?

   b. Which planet is warmer, Saturn or Pluto?

3. a. Are whales **cold-blooded** or **warm-blooded?**

   b. Are whales fish?

4. Tell the letter of the fish:

   a. with the **greatest** pressure on it.

   b. with the **least** pressure on it.

5. Name the muscle:

   a. on the **back** of the upper arm.

   b. on the **front** of the upper arm.

6. Name the arm muscle that gets shorter:

   a. when you straighten your arm.

   b. when you bend your arm.

7. In which form of matter do molecules:

   a. move fastest?

   b. move slowest?

8. Answer these questions about the galaxy we live in.

   a. What is its name?

   b. How many stars are in it?

9. In which form of matter are molecules:

   a. farthest apart?

   b. closest together?

10. Tell where a balloon would be **smaller:**

    a. at the surface of the ocean or 40 feet deep?

    b. 60 feet deep or 30 feet deep?

11. Name all the things in the list below that are matter in the liquid form.

    - air
    - milk
    - rock
    - tea
    - steam
    - water
    - wood
    - glass

12. As you touch each letter, say the letter. Then name the animal.

A

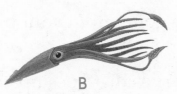
B

C

2. a. If you cut the nerve going from your foot to your brain, you could not ▮▮▮ your foot.

    b. If you cut the nerve going from your brain to your foot, you could not ▮▮▮ your foot.

3. Name the bundle of nerves that goes up and down through the middle of your backbone.

4. Name the part of the eye:

    a. where pictures are formed.

    b. where light enters the eyeball.

    c. that bends the light.

5. a. How many chambers does the heart have?

    b. How many chambers does the blood go through **before** it goes to the lungs?

    c. How many chambers does the blood go through **after** it goes to the lungs?

6. Say **big** or **small** to tell in which part of your ear chamber you would pick up each sound.

    a. very high voice

    b. low voice

7. a. Where does black blood go after it leaves the heart?

    b. Then the blood goes to the ▮▮▮.

    c. Then the blood goes to the ▮▮▮.

8. a. What color is blood that has fresh oxygen?

    b. What color is blood that does not have fresh oxygen?

    c. Where does blood pick up fresh oxygen?

9. a. How many bones are in the human body?

    b. Name the two things that bones do.

10. a. Things can't burn without ████.

    b. In the lungs, the color of blood changes from ████ to ████.

11. What's strange about:

    a. the bones in your backbone?

    b. the images in your eye?

12. a. Which part of your brain works when you think?

    b. To which part of the brain do the nerves from the eye go?

2. a. Which dinosaur lived earlier, Plateosaurus or Tyrannosaurus?

    b. About how long was Plateosaurus?

3. a. About how deep is the snow at the North Pole?

    b. How many hours does it take the sun to make a full circle around a person at the North Pole?

4. What's under the snow:

    a. at the North Pole?

    b. at the South Pole?

5. What part of a camera:

    a. bends the light that goes through it?

    b. lets just enough light into the camera?

6. Which letter shows:

    a. the film?

    b. the lens?

    c. the iris?

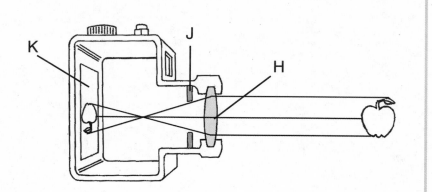

7. Say **toward** or **away from** for each blank.

During our winter, the North Pole tilts ▇▇▇ the sun and the South Pole tilts ▇▇▇ the sun.

8. a. What is part X?

  b. What is part Y?

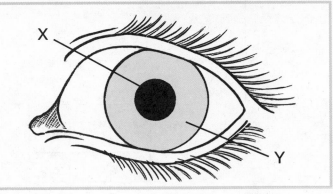

9. Tell if the hole in the iris is **big** or **small:**

  a. when things are very bright.

  b. when there's not much light.

10. As you touch animals **A, B** and **C,** say the letter. Then name the animal.

11. As you touch animals **D** and **E,** say the letter. Then name the animal.

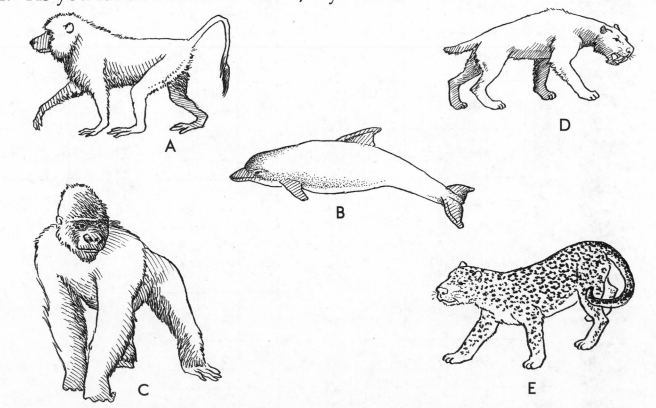

12. a. What are the 2 kinds of seasons that Africa has?

  b. Dinosaurs lived during the ▊▊▊.

Fact Game Scorecards

Lesson 10

1	2	3	4	5
6	7	8	9	10
11	12	13	14	15
16	17	18	19	20

Lesson 20

1	2	3	4	5
6	7	8	9	10
11	12	13	14	15
16	17	18	19	20

Lesson 30

1	2	3	4	5
6	7	8	9	10
11	12	13	14	15
16	17	18	19	20

Lesson 40

1	2	3	4	5
6	7	8	9	10
11	12	13	14	15
16	17	18	19	20

Lesson 50

1	2	3	4	5
6	7	8	9	10
11	12	13	14	15
16	17	18	19	20

Lesson 60

1	2	3	4	5
6	7	8	9	10
11	12	13	14	15
16	17	18	19	20

Lesson 70

1	2	3	4	5
6	7	8	9	10
11	12	13	14	15
16	17	18	19	20

Name _____

Fact Game Scorecards

Lesson 80

1	2	3	4	5
6	7	8	9	10
11	12	13	14	15
16	17	18	19	20

Lesson 90

1	2	3	4	5
6	7	8	9	10
11	12	13	14	15
16	17	18	19	20

Lesson 100

1	2	3	4	5
6	7	8	9	10
11	12	13	14	15
16	17	18	19	20

Lesson 110

1	2	3	4	5
6	7	8	9	10
11	12	13	14	15
16	17	18	19	20

Lesson 120

1	2	3	4	5
6	7	8	9	10
11	12	13	14	15
16	17	18	19	20

Lesson 130

1	2	3	4	5
6	7	8	9	10
11	12	13	14	15
16	17	18	19	20

Lesson 140

1	2	3	4	5
6	7	8	9	10
11	12	13	14	15
16	17	18	19	20

APPENDIX H—GROUP SUMMARY CHART

Teacher _____   **Reading Mastery Plus**   Group_____
                                        Level 4

Lessons	__1	__2	__3	__4	CO__5		__6	__7	__8	__9	CO/Test __	
Main Story Errors												
Name	IW	IW	IW	IW	CO	IW	IW	IW	IW	IW	CO	Test

Reading Checkout lessons

Teacher __Ms. Turner__   **Reading Mastery Plus**
                                         Level 4   Group __2__

Independent Work

Lessons	4 1	4 2	4 3	4 4	CO 4 5	4 6	4 7	4 8	4 9	CO/Test 5	
Main Story Errors	11	12	10	12	(16)	11	10	14	12	■	
Name	IW	IW	IW	IW	CO	IW	IW	IW	IW	IW	CO	Test
Luis Cepeda	2	1	2	1	P / 0	2	1	0	1	3	P / 0	2
Yoko Higashi	(4)	3	2	2	P / 0	2	3	1	2	2	P / 1	2
Anita Diaz	1	1	1	0	P / 0	2	1	1	0	2	P / 0	0
Denise Barton	1	2	0	1	(F) / 1	1	0	1	0	2	P / 2	(5)
Zachary Gray	1	0	0	1	P / 0	1	2	1	1	1	P / 0	0
Eric Adler	2	1	1	0	P / 1	1	0	1	0	2	P / 1	2

For all categories, circle any non-passing mark.

Main Story Errors Record number of errors group makes during main-story reading.

Independent Work (IW) Record number of errors. Passing criterion: 3 or fewer errors.

Reading Checkouts (CO) Record number of errors in lower part of box. Record P or F in upper part of box. Passing (P) is 100 (or more) wpm with 2 or fewer errors.

Test Record number of errors. See Test Summary Sheet (Appendix I) for passing criteria.

For more details, see pages 42, 57, 60, and 67 of this guide.

APPENDIX I – TEST SUMMARY SHEET

Name	Test 1	Test 2	Test 3	Test 4	Test 5	Test 6	Test 7

(Each test column contains a grid of numbered item boxes for recording student results. Test 1: items 1–35; Test 2: items 1–29; Test 3: items 1–36; Test 4: items 1–18; Test 5: items 1–34; Test 6: items 1–36; Test 7: items 1–36.)

Passing Criterion	32/35	26/29	32/36	16/18	31/34	32/36	32/36

APPENDIX I – TEST SUMMARY SHEET

Name	Test 8	Test 9	Test 10	Test 11	Test 12	Test 13	Test 14
	1 2 3 4 5 6 7 8 9 10 11 12 13 14 15 16 17 18 19 20 21 22 23 24 25 26	1 2 3 4 5 6 7 8 9 10 11 12 13 14 15 16 17 18 19 20 21 22 23 24 25 26 27 28 29 30 31 32 33 34 35 36	1 2 3 4 5 6 7 8 9 10 11 12 13 14 15 16 17 18 19 20 21 22 23 24 25 26 27 28 29 30 31 32 33 34	1 2 3 4 5 6 7 8 9 10 11 12 13 14 15 16 17 18 19 20 21 22 23 24 25 26 27 28 29 30 31 32 33 34 35 36	1 2 3 4 5 6 7 8 9 10 11 12 13 14 15 16 17 18 19 20 21 22 23 24 25 26 27 28 29 30	1 2 3 4 5 6 7 8 9 10 11 12 13 14 15 16 17 18 19 20 21 22 23 24 25 26 27 28	1 2 3 4 5 6 7 8 9 10 11 12 13 14 15 16 17 18 19 20 21 22 23 24 25 26 27 28 29 30 31 32 33 34 35
	1 2 3 4 5 6 7 8 9 10 11 12 13 14 15 16 17 18 19 20 21 22 23 24 25 26	1 2 3 4 5 6 7 8 9 10 11 12 13 14 15 16 17 18 19 20 21 22 23 24 25 26 27 28 29 30 31 32 33 34 35 36	1 2 3 4 5 6 7 8 9 10 11 12 13 14 15 16 17 18 19 20 21 22 23 24 25 26 27 28 29 30 31 32 33 34	1 2 3 4 5 6 7 8 9 10 11 12 13 14 15 16 17 18 19 20 21 22 23 24 25 26 27 28 29 30 31 32 33 34 35 36	1 2 3 4 5 6 7 8 9 10 11 12 13 14 15 16 17 18 19 20 21 22 23 24 25 26 27 28 29 30	1 2 3 4 5 6 7 8 9 10 11 12 13 14 15 16 17 18 19 20 21 22 23 24 25 26 27 28	1 2 3 4 5 6 7 8 9 10 11 12 13 14 15 16 17 18 19 20 21 22 23 24 25 26 27 28 29 30 31 32 33 34 35
	1 2 3 4 5 6 7 8 9 10 11 12 13 14 15 16 17 18 19 20 21 22 23 24 25 26	1 2 3 4 5 6 7 8 9 10 11 12 13 14 15 16 17 18 19 20 21 22 23 24 25 26 27 28 29 30 31 32 33 34 35 36	1 2 3 4 5 6 7 8 9 10 11 12 13 14 15 16 17 18 19 20 21 22 23 24 25 26 27 28 29 30 31 32 33 34	1 2 3 4 5 6 7 8 9 10 11 12 13 14 15 16 17 18 19 20 21 22 23 24 25 26 27 28 29 30 31 32 33 34 35 36	1 2 3 4 5 6 7 8 9 10 11 12 13 14 15 16 17 18 19 20 21 22 23 24 25 26 27 28 29 30	1 2 3 4 5 6 7 8 9 10 11 12 13 14 15 16 17 18 19 20 21 22 23 24 25 26 27 28	1 2 3 4 5 6 7 8 9 10 11 12 13 14 15 16 17 18 19 20 21 22 23 24 25 26 27 28 29 30 31 32 33 34 35
	1 2 3 4 5 6 7 8 9 10 11 12 13 14 15 16 17 18 19 20 21 22 23 24 25 26	1 2 3 4 5 6 7 8 9 10 11 12 13 14 15 16 17 18 19 20 21 22 23 24 25 26 27 28 29 30 31 32 33 34 35 36	1 2 3 4 5 6 7 8 9 10 11 12 13 14 15 16 17 18 19 20 21 22 23 24 25 26 27 28 29 30 31 32 33 34	1 2 3 4 5 6 7 8 9 10 11 12 13 14 15 16 17 18 19 20 21 22 23 24 25 26 27 28 29 30 31 32 33 34 35 36	1 2 3 4 5 6 7 8 9 10 11 12 13 14 15 16 17 18 19 20 21 22 23 24 25 26 27 28 29 30	1 2 3 4 5 6 7 8 9 10 11 12 13 14 15 16 17 18 19 20 21 22 23 24 25 26 27 28	1 2 3 4 5 6 7 8 9 10 11 12 13 14 15 16 17 18 19 20 21 22 23 24 25 26 27 28 29 30 31 32 33 34 35
	1 2 3 4 5 6 7 8 9 10 11 12 13 14 15 16 17 18 19 20 21 22 23 24 25 26	1 2 3 4 5 6 7 8 9 10 11 12 13 14 15 16 17 18 19 20 21 22 23 24 25 26 27 28 29 30 31 32 33 34 35 36	1 2 3 4 5 6 7 8 9 10 11 12 13 14 15 16 17 18 19 20 21 22 23 24 25 26 27 28 29 30 31 32 33 34	1 2 3 4 5 6 7 8 9 10 11 12 13 14 15 16 17 18 19 20 21 22 23 24 25 26 27 28 29 30 31 32 33 34 35 36	1 2 3 4 5 6 7 8 9 10 11 12 13 14 15 16 17 18 19 20 21 22 23 24 25 26 27 28 29 30	1 2 3 4 5 6 7 8 9 10 11 12 13 14 15 16 17 18 19 20 21 22 23 24 25 26 27 28	1 2 3 4 5 6 7 8 9 10 11 12 13 14 15 16 17 18 19 20 21 22 23 24 25 26 27 28 29 30 31 32 33 34 35
	1 2 3 4 5 6 7 8 9 10 11 12 13 14 15 16 17 18 19 20 21 22 23 24 25 26	1 2 3 4 5 6 7 8 9 10 11 12 13 14 15 16 17 18 19 20 21 22 23 24 25 26 27 28 29 30 31 32 33 34 35 36	1 2 3 4 5 6 7 8 9 10 11 12 13 14 15 16 17 18 19 20 21 22 23 24 25 26 27 28 29 30 31 32 33 34	1 2 3 4 5 6 7 8 9 10 11 12 13 14 15 16 17 18 19 20 21 22 23 24 25 26 27 28 29 30 31 32 33 34 35 36	1 2 3 4 5 6 7 8 9 10 11 12 13 14 15 16 17 18 19 20 21 22 23 24 25 26 27 28 29 30	1 2 3 4 5 6 7 8 9 10 11 12 13 14 15 16 17 18 19 20 21 22 23 24 25 26 27 28	1 2 3 4 5 6 7 8 9 10 11 12 13 14 15 16 17 18 19 20 21 22 23 24 25 26 27 28 29 30 31 32 33 34 35
	1 2 3 4 5 6 7 8 9 10 11 12 13 14 15 16 17 18 19 20 21 22 23 24 25 26	1 2 3 4 5 6 7 8 9 10 11 12 13 14 15 16 17 18 19 20 21 22 23 24 25 26 27 28 29 30 31 32 33 34 35 36	1 2 3 4 5 6 7 8 9 10 11 12 13 14 15 16 17 18 19 20 21 22 23 24 25 26 27 28 29 30 31 32 33 34	1 2 3 4 5 6 7 8 9 10 11 12 13 14 15 16 17 18 19 20 21 22 23 24 25 26 27 28 29 30 31 32 33 34 35 36	1 2 3 4 5 6 7 8 9 10 11 12 13 14 15 16 17 18 19 20 21 22 23 24 25 26 27 28 29 30	1 2 3 4 5 6 7 8 9 10 11 12 13 14 15 16 17 18 19 20 21 22 23 24 25 26 27 28	1 2 3 4 5 6 7 8 9 10 11 12 13 14 15 16 17 18 19 20 21 22 23 24 25 26 27 28 29 30 31 32 33 34 35
	1 2 3 4 5 6 7 8 9 10 11 12 13 14 15 16 17 18 19 20 21 22 23 24 25 26	1 2 3 4 5 6 7 8 9 10 11 12 13 14 15 16 17 18 19 20 21 22 23 24 25 26 27 28 29 30 31 32 33 34 35 36	1 2 3 4 5 6 7 8 9 10 11 12 13 14 15 16 17 18 19 20 21 22 23 24 25 26 27 28 29 30 31 32 33 34	1 2 3 4 5 6 7 8 9 10 11 12 13 14 15 16 17 18 19 20 21 22 23 24 25 26 27 28 29 30 31 32 33 34 35 36	1 2 3 4 5 6 7 8 9 10 11 12 13 14 15 16 17 18 19 20 21 22 23 24 25 26 27 28 29 30	1 2 3 4 5 6 7 8 9 10 11 12 13 14 15 16 17 18 19 20 21 22 23 24 25 26 27 28	1 2 3 4 5 6 7 8 9 10 11 12 13 14 15 16 17 18 19 20 21 22 23 24 25 26 27 28 29 30 31 32 33 34 35
Passing Criterion	23/26	32/36	31/34	32/36	27/30	25/28	32/35

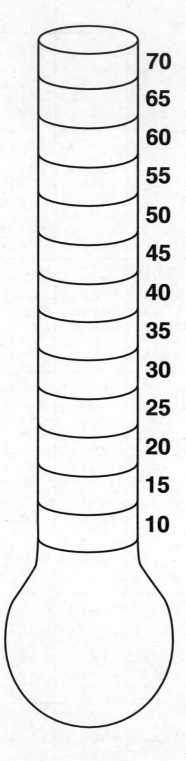

70

65

60

55

50

45

40

35

30

25

20

15

10

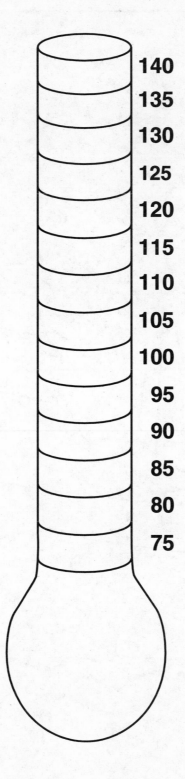

APPENDIX K—Map for Special Project After Lesson 10

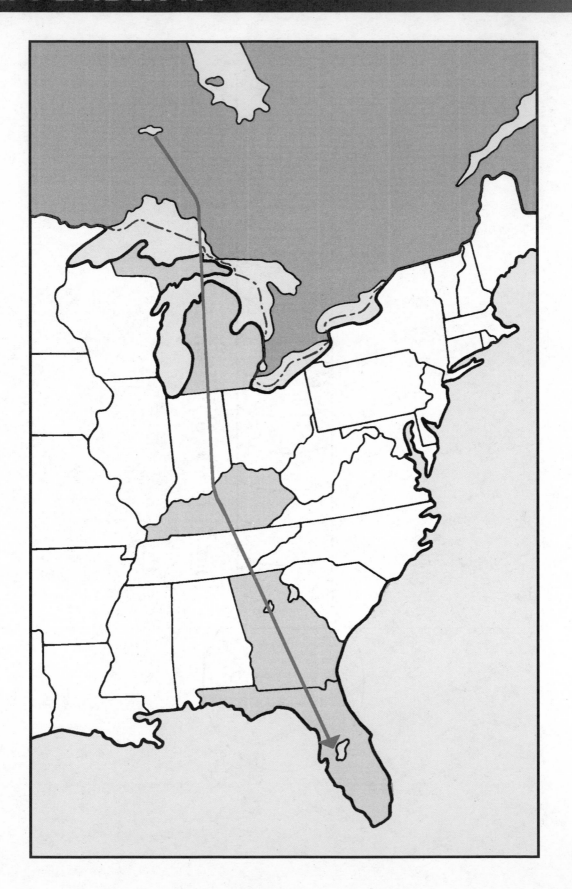

Level 4, Letter 1

To the family of _____

This school year your child is enrolled in the *Reading Mastery Plus* program. *Reading Mastery Plus,* Level 4 will help your child continue to improve upon the reading skills needed to succeed in school. Faster reading and more accurate word identification are two big areas your child will work on this year. Also, more silent reading practice will help your child become a better independent reader. Your child will be involved in research activities that require finding, reading, and using information to answer questions. And best of all, your child will learn about reading and why it is a useful tool that brings success in school work and enjoyment beyond the classroom.

In *Reading Mastery Plus,* Level 4, your child will continue to develop the ability to "read to learn." That means your child will be able to read with better understanding in subjects such as science and social studies. In addition, your child will work on important writing and language arts skills.

The best thing you can do this year is to let your child know that the work done in *Reading Mastery Plus,* Level 4 is very important. Encourage your child to read something at home every day. Remind your child "the more you read, the better reader you will be."

If you have any questions or want more ideas about how to help your child with reading this year, please call me at the school. I'll be happy to talk with you.

Thank you,

_____

Para la familia de _____

Este año escolar su hijo está inscrito en el programa *Reading Mastery Plus. Reading Mastery Plus,* Nivel 4 ayudará a su hijo a mejorar sus destrezas de lectura necesarias para triunfar en la escuela. Dos áreas importantes en las que su hijo trabajará este año son lectura más rápida e identificación de palabras más precisa. También la práctica de la lectura en silencio ayudará a su hijo a ser un mejor lector independiente. Su hijo estará involucrado en actividades de investigación que requerirán búsqueda, lectura y uso de información para responder preguntas. Y lo mejor de todo es que su hijo aprenderá acerca de la lectura y por qué es una herramienta útil que lleva al éxito en el trabajo escolar y del placer más allá del salón de clases.

En *Reading Mastery Plus,* Nivel 4, su hijo continuará desarrollando la destreza de "leer para aprender". Eso significa que su hijo podrá leer con un mejor entendimiento en materias como ciencias y estudios sociales. Además trabajará en destrezas de escritura y artes del lenguaje importantes.

Lo mejor que usted puede hacer este año es dejar que su hijo sepa que el trabajo que hace en *Reading Mastery Plus,* Nivel 4, es muy importante. Anímelo a leer algo en la casa diariamente. Recuérdele a su hijo que "mientras más lea, un mejor lector será".

Si tiene alguna pregunta o quiere más ideas acerca de cómo ayudar a su hijo con la lectura este año, por favor llámeme a la escuela. Me encantará hablar con usted.

Gracias,

_____

To the family of _____

    Your child has completed _____ lessons of *Reading Mastery Plus,* Level 4. Every day your child has worked on skills needed to read faster and more accurately. Your child is now a better independent reader and is able to find, read, and use information to answer questions and complete research assignments in other school subjects. These are important skills that will lead to success next year in school and in all the years to come.

    During this break in the school year, encourage your child to read something every day. Remind your child "the more you read, the better reader you will be." Tell your child you are proud of the progress made in school.

    If you have any questions or want more ideas about how to help your child with reading during this break in the school year, please call me at the school. I'll be happy to talk with you.

Thank you,

_____

Para la familia de _____

　　　Su hijo ha terminado _____ lecciones de *Reading Mastery Plus,* Nivel 4. Cada día su hijo ha trabajado en las destrezas necesarias para leer más rápido y con más precisión. Su hijo es ahora un mejor lector independiente y puede encontrar, leer y utilizar información para responder preguntas y completar trabajos de investigación en otras materias. Éstas son destrezas importantes que conducirán al éxito en el próximo año escolar y en los años venideros.

　　　Durante este receso del año escolar, anime a su hijo a leer algo diariamente. Recuérdele que "mientras más lea, un mejor lector será". Dígale que usted está orgulloso de su progreso en la escuela.

　　　Si usted tiene preguntas o quiere más ideas acerca de cómo ayudar a su hijo con la lectura durante este receso del año escolar, por favor llámeme a la escuela. Me encantará hablar con usted.

Gracias,

_____

APPENDIX M—SAMPLE LESSON

A

1	**2**	**3**
1. mukluks	1. gulped	1. rose
2. wrist	2. gently	2. sight
3. hailstone	3. owed	3. marble
4. playfully	4. wavy	4. dove
	5. kneeled	
	6. dents	

B

Facts About Clouds

You have read about a big storm cloud. Here are facts about clouds:

• Clouds are made up of tiny drops of water.

• In clouds that are very high, the water drops are frozen. Here is how those clouds look.

Picture 2

Picture 1

• Some clouds are storm clouds. They are flat on the bottom, but they go up very high. Sometimes they are five miles high.

• Some kinds of clouds may bring days of bad weather. These are low, flat clouds that look like bumpy blankets.

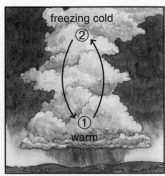
Picture 3

104   *Lesson 21*

The arrows in picture 3 show how the winds move inside a storm cloud. The winds move water drops to the top of the cloud. The drops freeze. When a drop freezes, it becomes a tiny hailstone. The tiny hailstone falls to the bottom of the cloud. At the bottom of the cloud, the tiny hailstone gets covered with more water. Then it goes up again and freezes again. Now the hailstone is a little bigger. It keeps going around and around in the cloud until it gets so heavy that it falls from the cloud. Sometimes it is as big as a baseball. Sometimes it is smaller than a marble.

If you want to see how many times a hailstone has gone to the top of the cloud, break the hailstone in half. You'll see rings. Each ring shows one trip to the top of the cloud. Count the rings and you'll know how many times the hailstone went through the cloud. Hailstone A went through the cloud three times.

How many times did Hailstone B go through the cloud?

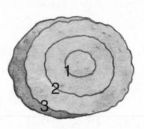

Hailstone A

Hailstone B

C The Killer Whales Wait

Oomoo took off one of her boots. She kneeled down and slammed the boot against the surface of the ice. The boot made a loud spanking sound. Oolak watched for a moment, then took off one of his boots and slapped it against the surface of the ice. "Maybe they'll hear this," Oomoo said. "I hope they do," she added. But she knew that it was still raining a little bit and that the rain made noise. She also knew that she and Oolak were far from shore—too far. They were more than a mile from the tent. She guessed that the sounds they made with their boots were lost in the rain and the slight breeze that was still blowing from the south.

From time to time, Oomoo glanced to the ocean. She hoped that she would see the killer whales moving far away. She hoped that the sound of the boots would scare them away. But each time she looked in their direction, she saw them moving back and forth, just past the top of the C-shaped ice floe.

Suddenly, Oolak tugged on Oomoo's shoulder and pointed toward the whales. His eyes were wide. He looked as if he was ready to cry. "I know," Oomoo said. Her voice was almost a whisper. "Just keep trying to signal," she said. "Maybe the people on the shore will hear us."

As she pounded her boot against the surface of the ice, she stared toward the shore. She wanted to see a kayak moving silently through the rain. She wanted to hear the signal of a bell ringing. She wanted to . . . .

Suddenly, she saw something white moving through the water. At first, she thought that it was a chunk of ice. But no, it couldn't be. It was not moving the way ice moves. It was very hard to tell what it was through the light rain. It wasn't a kayak. It wasn't a long boat. It was . . . Usk.

Usk ⭐ was swimming directly toward the ice chunk. And he was moving very fast.

"Usk!" Oomoo yelled as loudly as she could. "Usk!" She stood up and waved her arms.

The huge polar bear caught up to the ice chunk when it was not more than a hundred meters away from the killer whales. "Will they go after Usk?" Oolak asked.

"They'll go after Usk if they're hungry," Oomoo replied. "We've got to get out of here fast."

The huge bear swam up to the ice chunk, put his huge paws on the surface, and started to climb onto it. When he tried that, he almost tipped it over.

"No," Oomoo said. "Stay down." She tried to push him back. He rolled into the water and made a playful circle. "Give me your laces," Oomoo said to Oolak. Oomoo and Oolak untied the laces from their boots. These laces were long, thick straps of animal skin. Oomoo tied all the laces together. Quickly, she glanced back. The ice chunk was less than a hundred meters from the killer whales.

She called Usk. He playfully swam around the ice chunk, rolling over on his back and slapping the water with his front paws. Oomoo waited until Usk got close to the shore side of the ice chunk. Then she slipped the laces around his neck. "Hang on tight," she told Oolak, and handed him one end of the laces. She and Oolak sat down on the ice chunk and tried to dig their heels into dents in the surface of the ice.

"Play sled," she told Usk. "Play sled. Go home."

At first, Usk just rolled over and almost got the laces tangled in his front paws. "Home," Oomoo repeated. "Play sled and go home."

Usk stayed next to the ice chunk, making a playful sound. "Home," Oomoo shouted again.

Then Usk seemed to figure out what he was supposed to do. Perhaps he saw the fins of the killer whales. He got low in the water and started to swim toward shore.

D Number your paper from 1 through 12.

Story Items

1. What were Oomoo's boot laces made of?
2. What did Oomoo do with the laces after she tied them together?
3. What did she want Usk to do?
4. Did Usk immediately understand what he was supposed to do?
5. What did Usk start doing at the end of the story?

Review Items

6. The map shows a route. What state is at the north end of the route?

7. What country is at the south end of the route?

8. About how many miles is the route?

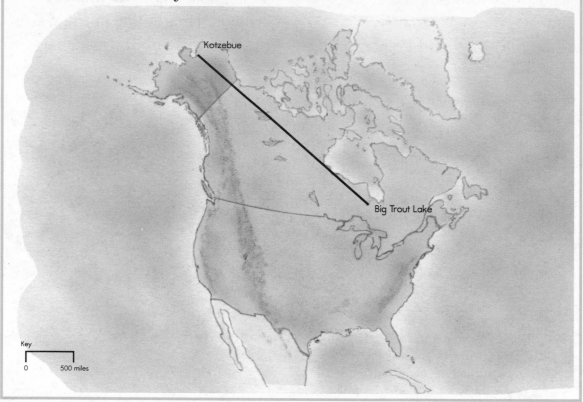

9. Female animals fight in the spring to protect ████.

10. Name 2 kinds of Alaskan animals that are dangerous in the spring.

11. Is it easier to fly alone or with a large flock?

12. Flying near the back of a large flock is like riding your bike ████.
    - with the wind   - against the wind

Name _____

21

A

1. What are clouds made of? _____

2. What kind of cloud does picture **A** show? _____

3. Write the letter of the clouds that may stay in the sky for days at a time. _____

4. Write the letter of the storm clouds. _____

5. Write the letter of the clouds that have frozen drops of water. _____

6. Write the letter of the clouds that may be five miles high. _____

7. Look at cloud A. At which number does a drop of water start? _____

8. What happens to the drop at the number **2**? _____

9. Draw 2 arrows on cloud **A** to show how a hailstone forms and returns to 1.

A

B

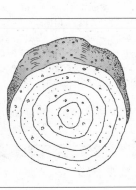

C

10. If you break a hailstone in half, what will you see inside the hailstone? _____

11. The picture shows half of a hailstone. How many times did the stone go through a cloud? _____

B   Story Items

12. Oomoo slapped her boot on the ice to make noise. Why did she want the people on shore to hear the noise? _____

13. Why did she want the killer whales to hear the noise? _____

14. Was Oomoo sure that someone would hear her? _____

15. About how far was the ice chunk from the tent? _____

16. About how far was the ice chunk from the killer whales? _____

Review Items

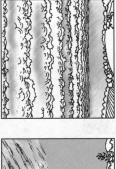

17. Write **north**, **south**, **east** and **west** in the correct boxes.

18. In which direction is ocean current **J** moving? _____

19. In which direction is ocean current **K** moving? _____

20. Which direction is the wind coming from? _____

21. Make an arrow above ice chunk **L** to show the direction the current will move the ice chunk.

22. Make an arrow above ice chunk **M** to show the direction the current will move the ice chunk.

GO TO PART D IN YOUR TEXTBOOK.

EXERCISE 1

VOCABULARY

a. **Find page 352 in your textbook.** ✓
- Touch sentence 4. ✓
- This is a new vocabulary sentence. It says: The smell attracted flies immediately. Everybody, say that sentence. Get ready. (**Signal.**) *The smell attracted flies immediately.*
- Close your eyes and say the sentence. Get ready. (**Signal.**) *The smell attracted flies immediately.*
- (Repeat until firm.)

b. The smell **attracted** flies. If the smell attracted flies, the smell really interested the flies and pulled them toward the smell. Everybody, what word means **really interested** the flies? (**Signal.**) *Attracted.*

c. The sentence says the smell attracted flies **immediately. Immediately** means **right now.** Everybody, what word means **right now?** (**Signal.**) *Immediately.*

d. Listen to the sentence again: The smell attracted flies immediately. Everybody, say that sentence. Get ready. (**Signal.**) *The smell attracted flies immediately.*

e. What word means **really interested** the flies? (**Signal.**) *Attracted.*
- What word means **right now?** (**Signal.**) *Immediately.*

EXERCISE 2

READING WORDS

Column 1

a. **Find lesson 21 in your textbook.** ✓
- Touch column 1. ✓
- (Teacher reference:)

1. mukluks	3. hailstone
2. wrist	4. playfully

b. Word 1 is **mukluks.** What word? (**Signal.**) *Mukluks.*
- Spell **mukluks.** Get ready. (**Tap for each letter.**) *M-U-K-L-U-K-S.*
- Mukluks are very warm boots that Eskimos wear.

c. Word 2 is **wrist.** What word? (**Signal.**) *Wrist.*
- Spell **wrist.** Get ready. (**Tap for each letter.**) *W-R-I-S-T.*
- Your wrist is the joint between your hand and your arm. Everybody, touch your wrist. ✓

d. Word 3. What word? (**Signal.**) *Hailstone.*

e. Word 4. What word? (**Signal.**) *Playfully.*

f. Let's read those words again, the fast way.
- Word 1. What word? (**Signal.**) *Mukluks.*
- (Repeat for words 2–4.)

g. (Repeat step f until firm.)

Column 2

h. **Find column 2.** ✓
- (Teacher reference:)

1. gulped	4. wavy
2. gently	5. kneeled
3. owed	6. dents

i. All these words have an ending.

j. Word 1. What word? (**Signal.**) *Gulped.*
- When you gulp something, you swallow it quickly. Here's another way of saying **She swallowed the water quickly: She gulped the water.**
- What's another way of saying **They swallowed their food quickly?** (**Signal.**) *They gulped their food.*
- Word 2. What word? (**Signal.**) *Gently.*
- Things that are gentle are the opposite of things that are rough. Everybody, what's the opposite of **a rough touch?** (**Signal.**) *A gentle touch.*
- What's the opposite of someone who behaves roughly? (**Signal.**) *Someone who behaves gently.*
- (Repeat until firm.)
- Word 3. What word? (**Signal.**) *Owed.*
- Something that you owe is something that you must pay. If you owe five dollars, you must pay five dollars. If you owe somebody a favor, you must pay that person a favor.

- Word 4. What word? (Signal.) *Wavy.*
- (Repeat for: **5. kneeled, 6. dents.**)

k. Let's read those words again, the fast way.
- Word 1. What word? (Signal.) *Gulped.*
- (Repeat for: **2. gently, 3. owed, 4. wavy, 5. kneeled, 6. dents.**)

l. (Repeat step k until firm.)

Column 3

m. Find column 3. ✓
- (Teacher reference:)

1. rose	3. marble
2. sight	4. dove

n. Word 1. What word? (Signal.) *Rose.*
- Something that moves up today rises. Something that moved up yesterday **rose.** Everybody, what do we say for something that moves up today? (Signal.) *Rises.*
- What do we say for something that moved up yesterday? (Signal.) *Rose.*
- Word 2. What word? *Sight.*
- A sight is something you see. A terrible sight is something terrible that you see. Everybody, what do we call something **wonderful** that you see? (Signal.) *A wonderful sight.*
- Word 3. What word? (Signal.) *Marble.*
- Word 4 rhymes with **stove.** What word? (Signal.) *Dove.*

o. Let's read those words again.
- Word 1. What word? (Signal.) *Rose.*
- (Repeat for words 2–4.)

p. (Repeat step o until firm.)

Individual Turns

(For columns 1–3: Call on individual students, each to read one to three words per turn.)

EXERCISE 3

COMPREHENSION PASSAGE

a. Find part B in your textbook. ✓
- You're going to read the next story about Oomoo and Oolak. First, you'll read the information passage. It gives some facts about clouds.

b. Everybody, touch the title. ✓
- (Call on a student to read the title.) [*Facts About Clouds.*]

- Everybody, what's the title? (Signal.) *Facts About Clouds.*

c. (Call on individual students to read the passage, each student reading two or three sentences at a time. Ask the specified questions as the students read.)

> **Facts About Clouds**
> You have read about a big storm cloud. Here are facts about clouds:
> Clouds are made up of tiny drops of water.

- Everybody, say that fact. Get ready. (Signal.) *Clouds are made up of tiny drops of water.*

> In clouds that are very high, the water drops are frozen. Here is how those clouds look.

Picture 1   Picture 2

- Everybody, in what kind of clouds are the water drops frozen? (Signal.) *In clouds that are very high.*
- Touch a high cloud. ✓
- Those clouds are very pretty in the sunlight because the light bounces off the tiny frozen drops.

> Some kinds of clouds may bring days of bad weather. These are low, flat clouds that look like bumpy blankets.

- Everybody, what kind of clouds may bring days of bad weather? (Signal.) *Low, flat clouds.*
- Does that kind of cloud pass over quickly? (Signal.) *No.*
- Touch a low, flat cloud. ✓
- How long may that kind of cloud be around? (Call on a student. Idea: *Days.*)

> Some clouds are storm clouds. They are flat on the bottom, but they go up very high. Sometimes they are five miles high.

- Tell me how a storm cloud looks. (Call on a student. Idea: *It's flat on the bottom and it goes up very high.*)
- Everybody, how high is the top of a big storm cloud sometimes? (Signal.) *Five miles.*

The arrows in picture 3 show how the winds move inside a storm cloud. The winds move water drops to the top of the cloud.

- Everybody, touch the number **1** that is inside the cloud. ✓
- That's where a drop of water starts. The wind blows it up to the top of the cloud. Everybody, follow the arrow to the top of the cloud and then stop. ✓
- Tell me about the temperature of the air at the top of the cloud. Get ready. (Signal.) *It's freezing cold.*
- So what's going to happen to the drop? (Call on a student. Idea: *It will freeze.*)

The drops freeze. When a drop freezes, it becomes a tiny hailstone.

- Everybody, what do we call a drop when it moves up and freezes? (Signal.) *A tiny hailstone.*

The tiny hailstone falls to the bottom of the cloud.

- Everybody, touch the number **2** in the cloud. ✓
- That's where the drop freezes. Now it falls down. Everybody, follow the arrow down. ✓
- What's the temperature like at the bottom of the cloud? (Signal.) *It's warm.*

At the bottom of the cloud, the tiny hailstone gets covered with more water. Then it goes up again and freezes again.

- Everybody, when it gets to the top of the cloud, what's going to happen to the water that is covering it? (Signal.) *It will freeze.*

Now the hailstone is a little bigger. It keeps going around and around in the cloud until it gets so heavy that it falls from the cloud. Sometimes it is as big as a baseball. Sometimes it is smaller than a marble.

- Everybody, touch the number **1** in the cloud. ✓
- Pretend that your finger is a drop. Show me a drop that goes around inside the cloud four times. Each time it goes through the top of the cloud, say: "It freezes." Go. ✓

If you want to see how many times a hailstone has gone to the top of the cloud, break the hailstone in half. You'll see rings.

- Everybody, what will you see inside the hailstone? (Signal.) *Rings.*

Each ring shows one trip to the top of the cloud. Count the rings and you'll know how many times the hailstone went through the cloud. Hailstone A went through the cloud three times.

- The rings are numbered. Everybody, count the rings in hailstone A out loud, starting with the center circle. Get ready. (Signal.) *One, two, three.*

How many times did Hailstone B go through the cloud?

- Everybody, figure out the answer. Remember to count the outside ring. (Wait.)
- How many times? (Signal.) *Seven.*

EXERCISE 4
STORY READING

a. Find part C in your textbook. ✓
- The error limit for group reading is 12 errors.
b. Everybody, touch the title. ✓
- (Call on a student to read the title.) *[The Killer Whales Wait.]*
- Everybody, what's the title? (Signal.) *The Killer Whales Wait.*

- Where were Oolak and Oomoo when we left them? (Call on a student. Idea: *Floating on an ice chunk.*)
c. (Call on individual students to read the story, each student reading two or three sentences at a time. Ask the specified questions as the students read.)

> - (Correct errors: Tell the word. Direct the student to reread the sentence.)
> - (If the group makes more than 12 errors, direct the students to reread the story.)

The Killer Whales Wait
Oomoo took off one of her boots. She kneeled down and slammed the boot against the surface of the ice.

- Why do you think she was doing that? (Call on a student. Idea: *She was trying to make noise so someone would hear her.*)
- Why didn't she yell? (Call on a student. Ideas: *She was losing her voice; nobody could hear her.*)

The boot made a loud spanking sound. Oolak watched for a moment, then took off one of his boots and slapped it against the surface of the ice. "Maybe they'll hear this," Oomoo said. "I hope they do," she added. But she knew that it was still raining a little bit and that the rain made noise. She also knew that she and Oolak were far from shore—too far. They were more than a mile from the tent. She guessed that the sounds they made with their boots were lost in the rain and the slight breeze that was still blowing from the south.

- Everybody, did she think that the people on the shore would hear the sounds? (Signal.) *No.*
- About how far away were these people? (Signal.) *Over a mile.*
- Why didn't she think they would hear the signal? (Call on a student. Idea: *Because the wind and rain were louder than the signal.*)

From time to time, Oomoo glanced to the ocean. She hoped that she would see the killer whales moving far away. She hoped that the sound

of the boots would scare them away. But each time she looked in their direction, she saw them moving back and forth, just past the top of the C-shaped ice floe.

- How do you think that made her feel? (Call on a student. Idea: *Afraid.*)

Suddenly, Oolak tugged on Oomoo's shoulder and pointed toward the whales. His eyes were wide. He looked as if he was ready to cry. "I know," Oomoo said.

- What does she mean when she says, "I know?" (Call on a student. Idea: *She knew the whales were there.*)

Her voice was almost a whisper. "Just keep trying to signal," she said. "Maybe the people on the shore will hear us."

- Everybody, had Oolak noticed the whales before? (Signal.) *No.*
- Why did he look as if he was ready to cry? (Call on a student. Idea: *Because he was afraid of the killer whales.*)

As she pounded her boot against the surface of the ice, she stared toward the shore. She wanted to see a kayak moving silently through the rain. She wanted to hear the signal of a bell ringing. She wanted to . . . .

- She stopped thinking about those things. I wonder why.

Suddenly, she saw something white moving through the water.

- What do you think it is? (Call on individual students. Ideas: *Another ice chunk; a boat; an animal;* etc.)

At first, she thought that it was a chunk of ice. But no, it couldn't be. It was not moving the way ice moves. It was very hard to tell what it was through the light rain. It wasn't a kayak. It wasn't a long boat. It was . . . Usk.

Usk ✦ was swimming directly toward the ice chunk. And he was moving very fast.

"Usk!" Oomoo yelled as loudly as she could. "Usk!" She stood up and waved her arms.

The huge polar bear caught up to the ice chunk when it was not more than a hundred meters away from the killer whales. "Will they go after Usk?" Oolak asked.

- Everybody, who does he think might go after Usk? (Signal.) *The killer whales.*
- How close are they to the whales now? (Call on a student. Idea: *About 100 meters.*)

"They'll go after Usk if they're hungry," Oomoo replied. "We've got to get out of here fast."

The huge bear swam up to the ice chunk, put his huge paws on the surface, and started to climb onto it. When he tried that, he almost tipped it over.

- Why? (Call on a student. Idea: *Because he was so heavy.*)

"No," Oomoo said. "Stay down." She tried to push him back. He rolled into the water and made a playful circle. "Give me your laces," Oomoo said to Oolak. Oomoo and Oolak untied the laces from their boots. These laces were long, thick straps of animal skin. Oomoo tied all the laces together. Quickly, she glanced back. The ice chunk was less than a hundred meters from the killer whales.

She called Usk. He playfully swam around the ice chunk, rolling over on his back and slapping the water with his front paws.

- What does Usk want to do? (Call on a student. Idea: *Play.*)

Oomoo waited until Usk got close to the shore side of the ice chunk.

- Everybody, which side did he move to? (Signal.) *The shore side.*

- What do you think Oomoo's going to do? (Call on a student. Idea: *Get Usk to help them get back to shore.*)

Then she slipped the laces around his neck. "Hang on tight," she told Oolak, and handed him one end of the laces. She and Oolak sat down on the ice chunk and tried to dig their heels into dents in the surface of the ice.

"Play sled," she told Usk. "Play sled. Go home."

- Read the rest of the story to yourself. Find out two things. Find out what Usk did at first. Find out something he may have seen that made him stop being playful. Raise your hand when you're done.

At first, Usk just rolled over and almost got the laces tangled in his front paws. "Home," Oomoo repeated. "Play sled and go home."

Usk stayed next to the ice chunk, making a playful sound. "Home," Oomoo shouted again.

Then Usk seemed to figure out what he was supposed to do. Perhaps he saw the fins of the killer whales. He got low in the water and started to swim toward shore.

- (After all students have raised their hands:)
- What did Oomoo keep telling Usk to do? (Call on a student. Ideas: *Go home; play sled.*)
- Everybody, did Usk do that at first? (Signal.) *No.*
- What did he do? (Call on a student. Idea: *Rolled over.*)
- What may Usk have seen that made him stop being playful? (Call on a student. Idea: *The fins of the killer whales.*)
- What did Usk do then? (Call on a student. Idea: *Swam toward shore.*)
- Everybody, look at the picture. What are Oomoo and Oolak hanging on to? (Signal.) *The laces.*
- Point on the picture to show the direction Usk is moving. ✓

EXERCISE 5

PAIRED PRACTICE

You're going to read aloud to your partner. Today the **B** members will read first. Then the **A** members will read from the star to the end of the story.
(Observe students and give feedback.)

End-of-Lesson Activities

INDEPENDENT WORK

Now finish your independent work for lesson 21. Raise your hand when you're finished. (Observe students and give feedback.)

WORKCHECK

a. (Direct students to take out their marking pencils.)
 • We're going to check your independent work. Remember, if you got an item wrong, make an **X** next to the item. Don't change any answers.

b. (For each item: Read the item. Call on a student to answer it. If the answer is wrong, say the correct answer. Refer to the Answer Key for the correct answers.)
c. Now use your marking pencil to fix up any items you got wrong. Remember, all mistakes must be fixed up before you hand in your independent work.

LANGUAGE ARTS

(Present Language Arts lesson 21 after completing Reading lesson 21. See Language Arts Guide.)

ACTIVITIES

(Present Activity 2 after completing Reading lessons 21. See Activities Across the Curriculum.)

Note: A special project occurs after lesson 22. See page 128 for the materials you'll need.

APPENDIX N– Behavioral Objectives

The *Reading Mastery Plus* program is based on the underlying concept that all students can learn if carefully taught. The program provides the kind of careful instruction that is needed to teach basic reading, literature, writing, and spelling skills.

The sequence of skills in *Reading Mastery Plus* Level 4 is controlled so that the student confidently performs the skills at each step before going on to more complicated tasks. The program builds on the skills developed in *Reading Mastery Plus* Level 3 and also teaches new concepts in the following areas:

Reading—reading vocabulary; story reading; comprehension readiness; vocabulary comprehension; story comprehension, literal and inferential; and reasoning skills.

Literary Skills—character traits and setting; and types of literature.

Study Skills—writing; using reference material; and following directions.

Literature—realistic fiction; fantasy; and novels.

Language Arts—writing; vocabulary; listening skills; speaking skills; and reference material.

Activities Across the Curriculum— activities in science; social studies; math; writing; and art.

In addition, students have an opportunity to improve and expand independent work skills through daily independent work. Comprehension is taught as students complete exercises related to stories or factual passages previously read. Language arts skills are practiced as students use these skills to complete worksheet activities.

Scope and Sequence

The Scope and Sequence on page 173 provides a quick overview of *Reading Mastery Plus* Level 4. The chart lists the various tracks (skills) that are taught and the range of lessons for each track.

Behavioral Objectives

This information gives a comprehensive picture of *Reading Mastery Plus* Level 4. It focuses on the general curriculum goals of the program and on special behavioral goals to be achieved by individual students.

The Behavioral Objectives, which begin on page 176, cover the major skill areas, or tracks, within each of the areas of Reading, Literary Skills, Study Skills, Literature Language Arts, and Activities Across the Curriculum shown on the Scope and Sequence. The chart is divided into four sections:

- The **Purpose of the track** is the general curriculum objective.

- The **Behavioral Objective** is the kind of performance that can be expected from the student who has mastered the skill.

- The section headed **The student is asked to** describes the specific kinds of tasks the student performs in order to master the skill.

- The section headed **First appears in** or **First appears after** shows where the skill is first introduced in the program.

Scope and Sequence

The following Scope and Sequence provides an overview of the skills taught in *Reading Mastery Plus* Level 4. The skills are divided into six principal areas: reading skills, literary skills, study skills, language arts skills, literature, and activities across the curriculum.

READING SKILLS

Decoding Skills
Words	1–140
Sentences and stories	1–140

Comprehension Skills
Readiness	1–140
Vocabulary	1–140
Literal comprehension	1–140
Interpretive comprehension	1–140
Reasoning	1–140

LITERARY SKILLS

Literary Skills
Characters and Setting	1–140

Types of literature
Realistic fiction	1–9, 11–19, 21–29, 31–39, 41–44, 46–49, 51–54, 71–74, 76–79, 81–89, 91–99
Fantasy	56–59, 61–64, 65–69, 101–109, 111–119, 121–129, 131–139

STUDY SKILLS

Study Skills
Writing	1–140
Using reference material	1–140

LANGUAGE ARTS SKILLS

Language Arts Skills
Writing	1–140
Vocabulary	68–124
Listening skills	8–140
Speaking skills	8–140
Reference material	18–113

ACTIVITIES ACROSS THE CURRICULUM

Activities Across the Curriculum	14–139

LITERATURE

Novels	after lesson 140
Literature Anthology	10–140 every tenth lesson plus lesson 135

Purpose of the track	Behavioral objectives	The student is asked to	Lesson range
DECODING SKILLS: WORDS To teach students to decode words.	When presented with a list of vocabulary words, the student reads the list without error.	Orally read lists of vocabulary words.	1–140
	When presented with a list of compound words, the student reads the list without error.	Orally read lists of compound words.	11–140
	When presented with a list of regularly spelled words, the student reads the list without error.	Orally read a list of regularly spelled words.	1–140
	When presented with a list of irregularly spelled words, the student reads the list without error.	Orally read a list of irregularly spelled words.	1–140
	When presented with a common word or phrase, the student reads the words without error.	Orally read a common word or phrase used in a *Textbook* selection.	1–140
	When presented with a list of words with endings, the student reads the words without error.	Orally read words with endings: s ly ion ing er en ed ish y ful ous ment ive est ness	Begins in lesson: 1 1 2 2 2 3 3 6 9 13 13 16 61 64 91
	When presented with a list of words with list of words with prefixes, the student reads the words without error.	Orally read words with prefixes: re ex	Begins in lesson: 78 116
	When presented with a list of multisyllable words, the student reads the list without error.	Orally read a list of multisyllable words.	8–140
	When presented with a list of hard words, the student reads the list without error.	Orally read a list of hard words.	1–140
	When presented with a hyphenated word, the student reads the word without error.	Read a hyphenated word correctly.	44, 52–140
	When presented with a list of science words the student reads the list without error.	Read a list of science words without error.	52–53, 59
	When presented with a possessive noun, the student reads the word without error.	Read a possessive noun correctly.	67–140
	When presented with contractions, the student reads the list without error.	Read contractions.	59–140

Teacher Presentation Book Lessons (continued)

DECODING SKILLS: SENTENCES AND STORIES To teach the student to use decoding skills to read sentences and stories	When presented with a reading selection, the student reads it aloud with a minimum of decoding errors.	Read part of a *Textbook* selection aloud.	1–140
	When presented with a reading selection, the student reads it silently.	Read part of a *Textbook* selection silently.	1–140
	When presented with a passage, the student reads it aloud within a specific time and decoding error limit.	Orally read a given passage in 1 minute or less with a minimum of decoding errors.	10–140 every fifth lesson
	When presented with a passage, the student engages in paired practice reading.	Orally engages in paired practice reading.	1–9 and all lessons except every fifth lesson
COMPREHENSION SKILLS: COMPREHENSION READINESS To teach the student to follow directions and answer comprehension questions	When given oral directions, the student follows them accurately.	Follow directions presented orally by the teacher.	1–140
	When presented with a picture, the student answers comprehension questions about it.	Answer comprehension questions about pictures in the *Textbook.*	1–140
COMPREHENSION SKILLS: VOCABULARY To teach the student the meanings of vocabulary words	When presented with a common word or phrase, the student explains what it means.	Explain the meaning of a common word or phrase used in a *Textbook* selection.	3–140
	When presented with a written definition of a word, the student comprehends the definition.	1. Read lists of vocabulary words.	3–140
		2. Answer questions about vocabulary words that the teacher defines orally.	3–140
		3. Answer questions about vocabulary words that are defined in writing.	35–140
	When presented with a vocabulary word, the student uses the word correctly within a sentence.	Use a vocabulary word correctly within a sentence.	5–140
	When presented with a vocabulary word, the student gives the opposite of the word.	Give a synonym for a vocabulary word.	17–140
	When presented with a sentence, the student uses context to predict the meaning of a word in the sentence.	Use sentence context to predict the meaning of a vocabulary word.	12–140
	When presented with a crossword puzzle, the student completes it.	Use vocabulary words to complete a crossword puzzle.	75–78, 81, 89, 93, 97, 101, 109, 111, 113, 118, 124, 128, 137
COMPREHENSION SKILLS: LITERAL COMPREHENSION To teach the student to respond to literal comprehension questions when reading.	When presented with literal questions about a reading selection, the student answers the questions.	Answer literal questions about a *Textbook* selection.	1–140
	After reading a selection, the student identifies literal causes and effects within the selection.	Answer questions about *Textbook* selection by identifying causes and effects.	1–140
	After reading a selection, the student recalls details and events from the selection.	Answer questions about a *Textbook* selection by recalling details and events.	1–140
	When presented with written directions, the student follows the directions.	Complete skill exercises by following written directions.	1–140
	After reading a story, the student puts events from the story in the correct order.	Put a list of events from a *Textbook* story in the correct order.	15–140

Teacher Presentation Book Lessons (continued)

COMPREHENSION SKILLS: INTERPRETIVE COMPREHENSION To teach the student to interpret what has been read	While reading a story, the student predicts a possible story outcome.	Predict the outcome of a *Textbook* story.	1–140
	When presented with a story title, the student predicts the content of the story.	Use a *Textbook* story's title as a basis for predicting its content.	1–140
	After reading a selection, the student infers causes and effects within the selection.	Answer questions about a *Textbook* selection by inferring causes and effects.	1–140
	After reading a selection, the student infers details and events within the selection.	Answer questions about a *Textbook* selection by inferring details and events.	1–140
	When presented with a paragraph, the student infers the main idea and the supporting details.	Read the main idea of a given paragraph and then infer three supporting details for the main idea.	1–140
COMPREHENSION SKILLS: REASONING To teach the student to use reasoning skills to respond to text	After reading a selection, the student draws conclusions based on evidence from the selection.	Answer questions about a *Textbook* selection by drawing conclusions.	1–140
	When presented with a fact, the student says the fact and answers questions based on the fact.	Repeat a fact and answer questions based on the fact.	1–140
	After reading a selection, the student evaluates problems and solutions within the selection.	Answer questions about a *Textbook* selection by evaluating problems and solutions.	1–140
LITERARY SKILLS: ANALYZING CHARACTERS AND SETTINGS To teach the student character traits and setting	After reading a story, the student names the character that a sentence describes.	Name the character that a sentence describes.	1–140
	After reading a story, the student interprets the feelings of a story character.	Answer questions about a *Textbook* story by interpreting a character's feelings.	1–140
	After reading a story, the student interprets the perspective of a story character.	Answer questions about a *Textbook* story by interpreting a character's perspective.	1–140
	After reading a story, the student plays the role of a story character.	Answer questions about a *Textbook* story by pretending to be a story character.	1–140
	After reading a story, the student interprets the motives of a story character.	Answer questions about a *Textbook* story by interpreting the character's motives.	1–140
	After reading a story, the student infers the point of view of a story character.	Answer questions about a *Textbook* story by inferring a character's point of view.	1–140
	After reading a story, the student predicts the actions of a story character.	Answer questions about a *Textbook* story by predicting a character's actions.	1–140
	After reading a story, the student identifies the important features of each story setting.	Answer questions about a *Textbook* story by distinguishing between settings.	1–140
	After reading a story, the student identifies the important traits of each story character.	Answer questions about a *Textbook* story by distinguishing between story characters.	1–140

Teacher Presentation Book Lessons (continued)

LITERARY SKILLS: TYPES OF LITERATURE To teach the student to read a variety of types of literature	When presented with realistic fiction, the student reads it.	Read realistic fiction in the *Textbook*.	1-9, 11-19, 21-29, 31-39, 41-44, 46-49, 51-54, 71-74, 76-79, 81-89, 91-99
	When presented with a comprehension passage, the student reads it.	Read a comprehension passage in the *Textbook*.	1-140
	When presented with a novel, the student reads it.	Read complete novels in the *Textbook*, and as part of the supplementary novel program found in the Literature Guide.	
	When presented with fantasy, the student reads it.	Read fantasy in the *Textbook*.	56-59, 61-64, 65-69, 101-109, 111-119, 121-129, 131-139
	When presented with factual and fictional selections, the student distinguishes between fact and fiction.	Complete exercises distinguishing between fact and fiction.	1-140
STUDY SKILLS: WRITING To teach the student to integrate writing and reading	When presented with a written question, the student writes the correct answer.	Write the answers to questions about a *Textbook* story.	1-140
	When presented with a specific writing assignment, the student completes the assignment.	Complete the daily writing assignments in the *Textbook*.	1-140
	After compiling information about a given topic, the student gives an oral presentation.	Present a completed special project.	12, 22-23, 35, 52-53, 67, 84, 107, 112, 117, 140
	After compiling information about a given topic, the student organizes the information into charts and other visual displays.	Complete special projects by drawing charts and other visual displays.	12, 22-23, 35, 52-53, 67, 84, 107, 112, 117, 140
STUDY SKILLS: USING REFERENCE MATERIALS To teach the student to use reference materials	When presented with a map, the student interprets it.	Use a given map to answer questions about a *Textbook* story about direction, relative size, proximity, labels, and other map-related concepts.	3-140
	When presented with a globe, the student interprets and responds to questions about it.	Interpret and answer questions about a globe.	56-140
	When presented with a timeline, the student interprets it.	Interpret a timeline.	54
	When presented with a CD-ROM, the student uses it to obtain information.	Use a given CD-ROM to obtain information.	12, 22-23, 35, 67, 107, 112, 117
	When presented with a diagram, the student interprets it.	Answer questions about a given diagram.	1-140
	When presented with an encyclopedia, the student uses it to gather information.	Complete activities by using an encyclopedia.	12, 22-23, 35, 67, 107, 112, 117
	When presented with the telephone directory yellow pages, the student uses it correctly.	Use the yellow pages in a phone book correctly.	49-51
	When presented with a special project, the student completes it.	Complete a special project.	12, 22-23, 35, 52-53, 67, 84, 107, 112, 117, 140

LITERATURE ANTHOLOGY

Purpose of the track	Behavioral objectives	The student is asked to	Lesson range
LITERATURE ANTHOLOGY To elaborate on skills student is learning and provide a wide genre of literature	The student reads and participates in activities related to each story in the Literature Anthology.	Read and participate in activities in the following literature selections: *The Velveteen Rabbit* *Dreams* *The Runner* *The Emperor's New Clothes* *Why Leopard Has Black Spots* *Boar Out There* *Crossing the Creek* *Camp on the High Prairie* *Spaghetti* *Charlie Best* *The Pancake Collector* *Not Just Any Ring* *A Lucky Thing* *The New Kid* *Steps* *The Soup Stone* *Julie Rescues Big Mack* *Amelia Bedelia* *My (Wow!) Summer Vacation* *The Story of Daedalus and Icarus*	First appears after lesson: 10 20 20 30 40 50 50 60 60 70 80 90 100 100 110 120 120 130 135 140

ACTIVITIES ACROSS THE CURRICULUM

Purpose of the track	Behavioral objectives	The student is asked to	Lesson range
ACTIVITIES ACROSS THE CURRICULUM To reinforce and extend the concepts and skills acquired in *Reading Mastery Plus* Level 4.	When presented with a content area activity, the student completes the activity.	Complete a content area activity.	14, 21, 23, 24, 33, 36, 41, 45, 48, 53, 56, 61, 64, 69, 74, 82, 86–89, 94, 105, 117, 119, 122–124, 126, 129, 132–134, 139

Purpose of the track	Behavioral objectives	The student is asked to	Lesson range
LANGUAGE ARTS To teach the student to write	When presented with a sentence, the student uses commas correctly.	Use commas correctly in a sentence: Commas in a series replacing *and*. Commas in a series replacing *or*. Commas in dates. Commas in addresses.	1–4 5–6 10–11 12–13
	When presented with the beginning of a sentence or a topic, the student completes the main idea and detail sentences.	Write a main idea and supporting detail sentences.	26–30, 34–39, 44, 50, 52, 57–59, 61–63, 66–67, 79, 80, 82, 102, 104–106, 108–109, 114, 116, 119, 121, 124, 126–127, 131, 133, 135, 137
	When presented with a subject, the student provides the correct verb agreement.	Write using correct subject-verb agreement.	40–43
	When presented with a topic, the student writes a multiparagraph story that infers and reports about a picture.	Write a story about a picture.	7, 9, 15, 16, 53, 55–56, 91, 93
	When presented with a previously written story, the student rewrites the story correcting all errors.	Edit and rewrite a previously written story.	7, 9, 15, 16, 53, 55–56, 91, 93
	When presented with a topic, the student writes a report.	Write a report on a given topic.	8, 14, 17, 54, 92
	When presented with a previously written report, the student rewrites the report correcting all errors.	Edit and rewrite a previously written report.	8, 14, 17, 54, 92
	When presented with a topic, the student writes from the perspective of someone else.	Write from the perspective of someone else.	45–49, 51, 60, 64–65, 81, 83, 101, 103, 107, 113, 115, 117–118, 122–123, 125, 128, 129–130, 132, 134, 136, 138–140
	When presented with a dictated passage, the student reconstructs it and writes an ending.	Reconstruct a dictated passage and write an ending.	90, 94
	When presented with a dictated passage, the student reconstructs it writes an ending and edits the passage.	Reconstruct, write an ending, and edit a dictated passage.	90, 94
	When presented with an incomplete outline and the main ideas for each paragraph, the student completes the outline.	Complete an outline from main ideas.	110–111
	When presented with an incomplete outline and the main idea, the student completes the outline.	Complete an outline from one major main idea.	112

Language Arts Lessons (continued)

LANGUAGE ARTS To teach the student vocabulary	When presented with an affix, the student identifies the meaning and uses it to make a new word.	Use the following affixes: dis re un less ful ness er super able mis ly	68–78, 86–87, 95 68–78, 85–89, 96 70–78, 85–89, 95 72–78, 84–85, 87–89, 95, 96 74–78, 84, 87, 89, 95 75–78, 84–89, 95, 96 77–78, 84–86, 89, 96 84–85 86–89, 96 88–89, 95, 96 95, 96
	When presented with words, the student identifies the root and affixes.	Identify root words and affixes.	97–100
	When presented with a multiple meaning word, the student uses a dictionary to identify the different meanings of the word.	Use a dictionary to identify the different meanings of a multiple meaning word.	113–114, 115–116
	When presented with a simile, the student explains the meaning.	Explain the meaning of a simile.	117–118, 120–121
	When presented with a metaphor, the student explains the meaning.	Explain the meaning of a metaphor.	119–121
	When presented with a word, the student writes words that alliterate.	Write words that alliterate.	122–124
LANGUAGE ARTS To teach the student listening skills	When a peer or teacher is speaking, the student exhibits good listening skills.	Repeat and exhibit good listening skills.	8, 14–140
LANGUAGE ARTS To teach the student speaking skills	After writing a group of sentences, report, or narrative, the student presents it to their peers.	Read a previously written group of sentences, report, or narrative.	8, 14–140
LANGUAGE ARTS To teach student to use reference material.	When presented with a reference source, the student uses it appropriately.	Use the following reference sources appropriately: Dictionary Encyclopedia Atlas	18–19, 23–25, 31–33, 40–42, 98–100, 113, 20–21, 23–25, 31–33, 40–42 22–25, 31–33, 40–42

APPENDIX O—Skills Profile Chart

Student's Name _____ Year _____

Teacher's Name _____

School's Name _____ Phone _____

Student's grade in school: _____

Number of days absent: lessons 1–50 _____   lessons 51–100 _____   lessons 101–140 _____

Last lesson completed _____   Date _____

Comments: _____

	Lessons 1–70	**Lessons 71–140**
Decoding Activities		
Story Reading		
Comprehension Activities		
Areas of Strength		
Areas of needed improvement		

Recommendations: _____

_____

Conference dates and results:

_____

_____

_____

_____

_____

CATEGORIES	SKILLS	APPEARS IN LESSONS	DATE MASTERED
DECODING SKILLS: WORDS	Orally read lists of vocabulary words.	1–140	
	Orally read lists of compound words.	11–140	
	Orally read a list of regularly spelled words.	1–140	
	Orally read a list of irregularly spelled words.	1–140	
	Orally read a common word or phrase used in a *Textbook* selection.	1–140	

	Orally read words with endings:
	  s
	  ly
	  ion
	  ing
	  er
	  en
	  ed
	  ish
	  y
	  ful
	  ous
	  ment
	  ive
	  est
	  ness
		Begins in lesson:
		1
		1
		2
		2
		2
		3
		3
		6
		9
		13
		13
		16
		61
		64
		91	

	Orally read words with prefixes:
	  re
	  ex
		Begins in lesson:
		78
		116	

	Orally read a list of multisyllable words.	8–140	
	Orally read a list of hard words.	1–140	
	Read a hyphenated word correctly	44, 52–140	
	Read a list of names of planets and moons without error.	52–53, 59	
	Read a possessive noun correctly.	67–140	
	Read contractions.	59–140	
DECODING SKILLS: SENTENCES AND STORIES	Read part of a *Textbook* selection aloud.	1–140	
	Read part of a *Textbook* selection silently.	1–140	
	Orally read a given passage in 1 minute or less with a minimum of decoding errors.	10–140 every fifth lesson	
	Orally engages in paired practice reading.	1–9 and all lessons except every fifth lesson	

Reading Activities (continued)

CATEGORIES	SKILLS	APPEARS IN LESSONS	DATE MASTERED
COMPREHENSION SKILLS: READINESS	Follow directions presented orally by the teacher.	1–140	
	Answer comprehension questions about pictures in the *Textbook*.	1–140	
COMPREHENSION SKILLS: VOCABULARY	Explain the meaning of a common word or phrase used in a *Textbook* selection.	3–140	
	Read lists of vocabulary words.	3–140	
	Answer questions about vocabulary words that the teacher defines orally.	3–140	
	Answer questions about vocabulary words that are defined in writing.	35–140	
	Use a vocabulary word correctly within a sentence.	5–140	
	Give a synonym for a vocabulary word.	17–140	
	Use sentence context to predict the meaning of a vocabulary word.	12–140	
	Use vocabulary words to complete a crossword puzzle.	75–78, 81, 89, 93, 97, 101, 109, 111, 113, 118, 124, 128, 137	
COMPREHENSION SKILLS: LITERAL COMPREHENSION	Answer literal questions about a *Textbook* selection.	1–140	
	Answer questions about *Textbook* selection by identifying causes and effects.	1–140	
	Answer questions about a *Textbook* selection by recalling details and events.	1–140	
	Complete skill exercises by following written directions.	1–140	
	Put a list of events from a *Textbook* story in the correct order.	15–140	
COMPREHENSION SKILLS: INTERPRETIVE COMPREHENSION	Predict the outcome of a *Textbook* story.	1–140	
	Use a *Textbook* story's title as a basis for predicting its content.	1–140	
	Answer questions about a *Textbook* selection by inferring causes and effects.	1–140	
	Answer questions about a *Textbook* selection by inferring details and events.	1–140	
	Read the main idea of a given paragraph and then infer three supporting details for the main idea.	1–140	
COMPREHENSION SKILLS: REASONING	Answer questions about a *Textbook* selection by drawing conclusions.	1–140	
	Repeat a fact and answer questions based on the fact.	1–140	
	Answer questions about a *Textbook* selection by evaluating problems and solutions.	1–140	

CATEGORIES	SKILLS	APPEARS IN LESSONS	DATE MASTERED
LITERARY SKILLS: CHARACTERS AND SETTING	Name the character that a sentence describes.	1–140	
	Answer questions about a *Textbook* story by interpreting a character's feelings.	1–140	
	Answer questions about a *Textbook* story by interpreting a character's perspective.	1–140	
	Answer questions about a *Textbook* story by pretending to be a story character.	1–140	
	Answer questions about a *Textbook* story by interpreting the character's motives.	1–140	
	Answer questions about a *Textbook* story by inferring a character's point of view.	1–140	
	Answer questions about a *Textbook* story by predicting a character's actions.	1–140	
	Answer questions about a *Textbook* story by distinguishing between settings.	1–140	
	Answer questions about a *Textbook* story by distinguishing between story characters.	1–140	
LITERARY SKILLS: TYPES OF LITERATURE	Read realistic fiction in the *Textbook*.	1–9, 11–19, 21–29, 31–39, 41–44, 46–49, 51–54, 71–74, 76–79, 81–89, 91–99	
	Read a comprehension passage in the *Textbook*.	1–140	
	Read complete novels in the *Textbook*, and as part of the supplementary novel program found in the Literature Guide.		
	Read fantasy in the *Textbook*.	56–59, 61–64, 65–69, 101–109, 111–119, 121–129, 131–139	
	Complete exercises distinguishing between fact and fiction.	1–140	

STUDY SKILLS

CATEGORIES	SKILLS	APPEARS IN LESSONS	DATE MASTERED
STUDY SKILLS: WRITING	Write the answers to questions about a *Textbook* story.	1–140	
	Complete the daily writing assignments in the *Textbook*.	1–140	
	Present a completed special project.	12, 22–23, 35, 52–53, 67, 84, 107, 112, 117, 140	
	Complete special projects by drawing charts and other visual displays.	12, 22–23, 35, 52–53, 67, 84, 107, 112, 117, 140	
STUDY SKILLS: USING REFERENCE MATERIAL	Use a given map to answer questions about a *Textbook* story about direction, relative size, proximity, labels, and other map-related concepts.	3–140	
	Interpret and answer questions about a globe.	56–140	
	Interpret a timeline.	54	
	Use a given CD-ROM to obtain information.	12, 22–23, 35, 67, 107, 112, 117	
	Answer questions about a given diagram.	1–140	
	Complete activities by using an encyclopedia.	12, 22–23, 35, 67, 107, 112, 117	
	Use the yellow pages in a phone book correctly.	49–51	
	Complete a special project.	12, 22–23, 35, 52–53, 67, 84, 107, 112, 117, 140	

LANGUAGE ARTS SKILLS

CATEGORIES	SKILLS	APPEARS IN LESSONS	DATE MASTERED
LANGUAGE ARTS: WRITING	Use commas correctly in a sentence: Commas in a series replacing *and*. Commas in a series replacing *or*. Commas in dates. Commas in addresses.	1–4 5–6 10–11 12–13	
	Write a main idea and supporting detail sentences.	26–30, 34–39, 44, 50, 52, 57–59, 61–63, 66–67, 79–80, 82, 102, 104–106, 108–109, 114, 116, 119, 121, 124, 126–127, 131, 133, 135, 137	

CATEGORIES	SKILLS	APPEARS IN LESSONS	DATE MASTERED
	Write using correct subject-verb agreement.	40–43	
	Write a story about a picture.	7, 9, 15, 16, 53, 55–56, 91, 93	
	Edit and rewrite a previously written story.	7, 9, 15, 16, 53, 55–56, 91, 93	
	Write a report on a given topic.	8, 14, 17, 54, 92	
	Edit and rewrite a previously written report.	8, 14, 17, 54, 92	
	Write from the perspective of someone else.	45–49, 51, 60, 64–65, 81, 83, 101, 103, 107, 113, 115, 117–118, 122–123, 125, 128, 129–130, 132, 134, 136, 138–140	
	Reconstruct a dictated passage and write an ending.	90, 94	
	Reconstruct, write an ending, and edit a dictated passage.	90, 94	
	Complete an outline from main ideas.	110–111	
	Complete an outline from one major main idea.	112	
LANGUAGE ARTS: VOCABULARY	Use the following affixes: dis re un less ful ness er super able mis ly	68–78, 86–87, 95 68–78, 85–89, 96 70–78, 85–89, 95 72–78, 84–85, 87–89, 95, 96 74–78, 84, 87, 89, 95 75–78, 84–89, 95, 96 77–78, 84–86, 89, 96 84–85 86–89, 96 88–89, 95, 96 95, 96	
	Identify root words and affixes.	97–100	
	Use a dictionary to identify the different meanings of a multiple meaning word.	113–114, 115–116	
	Explain the meaning of a simile.	117–118, 120–121	
	Explain the meaning of a metaphor.	119–121	
	Write words that alliterate.	122–124	
LANGUAGE ARTS: LISTENING SKILLS	Repeat and exhibit good listening skills.	8, 14–140	
LANGUAGE ARTS: SPEAKING SKILLS	Read a previously written group of sentences, report, or narrative.	8, 14–140	
LANGUAGE ARTS: REFERENCE MATERIAL	Use the following reference sources appropriately: Dictionary	18–19, 23–25, 31–33, 40–42, 98–100, 113	
	Encyclopedia	20–21, 23–25, 31–33, 40–42	
	Atlas	22–25, 31–33, 40–42	

ACTIVITIES ACROSS THE CURRICULUM

CATEGORIES	SKILLS	APPEARS IN LESSONS	DATE MASTERED
ACTIVITIES ACROSS THE CURRICULUM	Complete an activity in a content area.	14, 21, 23, 24, 33, 36, 41, 45, 48, 53, 56, 61, 64, 69, 74, 82, 86-89, 94, 105, 117, 119, 122-124, 126, 129, 132-134, 139	

LITERATURE

CATEGORIES	SKILLS	APPEARS IN LESSONS	DATE MASTERED
LITERATURE LESSONS	Read and participate in activities in the following literature selections:	First appears after lesson:	
	The Velveteen Rabbit	10	
	Dreams	20	
	The Runner	20	
	The Emperor's New Clothes	30	
	Why Leopard Has Black Spots	40	
	Boar Out There	50	
	Crossing the Creek	50	
	Camp on the High Prairie	60	
	Spaghetti	60	
	Charlie Best	70	
	The Pancake Collector	80	
	Not Just Any Ring	90	
	A Lucky Thing	100	
	The New Kid	100	
	Steps	110	
	The Soup Stone	120	
	Julie Rescues Big Mack	120	
	Amelia Bedelia	130	
	My (Wow!) Summer Vacation	135	
	The Story of Daedalus and Icarus	140